PRAISE FOR *WE WERE ONCE A FAMILY*

"*We Were Once a Family* fills in [a] crucial gap by tracing how two Texas sibling groups . . . came to be removed from their families and adopted by the Harts, even though the children had family members who were willing and able to take care of them . . . By meticulously showing how social workers, legal officials, and other authorities repeatedly failed the families, *We Were Once a Family* powerfully uses this one story . . . to expose how what happened to these children is indicative of the classism and racism still baked into the institution." —Kristen Martin, *The Atlantic*

"Roxanna Asgarian's tenacious and vulnerable reporting reveals the foundation of [the book's] intensely disturbing story—a broken child welfare system whose singular accomplishment has been the uniformity by which its bureaucracy has ruined lives across state lines . . . The book's transparency is our benefit and an informed invitation to step into the nature of family abuse . . . Asgarian's personalized fact finding provides essential context for understanding what happened . . . [and] compels us to listen and act." —Marcela Davison Avilés, NPR

"[*We Were Once a Family*] takes readers along Asgarian's five-year journey of interviews and investigative reporting . . . With fiercely empathetic narrative journalism reminiscent of journalist Svetlana Alexievich, Asgarian herself only appears in moments in which the adoptees and biological families' narratives are enhanced . . . [*We Were Once a Family*] is surely a book that should be included in curriculums for courses on social justice, social work and journalism." —Michelle Kicherer, *San Francisco Chronicle*

"The flood of stories that followed the murder-suicide largely revolved around the psychological motivations of the Hart women. But Texas-based reporter Roxanna Asgarian was interested in different questions . . . Asgarian went on to spend the next five years investigating the parts of the tragedy obscured by true-crime sensationalism . . . Her work refocuses the lens on the birth families who were painfully shut out of their children's lives and deaths."

—Bindu Bansinath, *The Cut*

"[Asgarian] has written a narrative so powerful, populated by people who are so vivid, that it can't be ignored, much less forgotten . . . [*We Were Once a Family*] is a reconstruction of a harrowing journey with no happy ending, one that challenges conventional assumptions at every turn and exposes the racist and economic biases of family courts."

—Mimi Swartz, *Texas Monthly*

"Roxanna Asgarian reveals far more than details of that shocking crash—delving deep into the human and systemic failures that preceded the horrifying murder-suicide in a new nonfiction book that's both riveting and deeply disturbing . . . More than an exposé, Asgarian's first book weaves a complex tale that brings those six lost Texas children's families into sharp and intimate focus. A crisp, colorful, and authoritative writer, she reveals difficult-to-obtain details . . . This deeply told tale is brimming with compassion for the children and for their families, as well as hard-hitting and vitally important investigative insights and analysis of the system that failed them all."

—Lise Olsen, *Texas Observer*

"Asgarian debuts with a comprehensive and searing look at systemic issues within the foster care and adoption systems . . . Emotional and frequently enraging, it adds up to a blistering indictment . . . Sensitive, impassioned, and eye-opening, this is a must-read."

—*Publishers Weekly* (starred review)

"A searching examination . . . Asgarian clearly shows how [a] dysfunctional system hinges on racist assumptions . . . Entirely convincing . . . A sobering call to action."

—*Kirkus Reviews*

"Roxanna Asgarian's stunning debut paints a stark picture of the systemic failures of our child welfare system. Asgarian shows the myriad ways in which the very institutions charged with our children's safety often exacerbate their predicaments. This book is sobering, but also urgent, advocating for change with the strength of a howl in the wild."

—Rachel Louise Snyder, author of *No Visible Bruises: What We Don't Know About Domestic Violence Can Kill Us*

"Roxanna Asgarian could have written another sensational account of the six Black children murdered by the white couple who adopted them. Instead, *We Were Once a Family* is not only the most in-depth investigation of the tragedy, but also a devastating exposé of the unjust and inhumane child welfare system that caused it to happen. This riveting book will raise public awareness of the urgent need to end our disastrous approach to struggling families by radically reimagining child welfare policies and building community-based supports that truly keep children safe."

—Dorothy Roberts, author of *Torn Apart*

"Roxanna Asgarian is one of our most important reporters working today, covering crime, the courts, and child welfare with boundless empathy, journalistic rigor, and unforgettable prose. *We Were Once a Family* shines a necessary light on all the systemic forces that made a seemingly unthinkable family tragedy all too preventable—and thus all the more infuriating. This book astonished me."

—Sarah Weinman, author of *The Real Lolita* and *Scoundrel*

"After Jennifer and Sarah Hart plunged themselves and their six children over a cliff in California, something strange happened: the media focused almost entirely on these white mothers, leaving the stories of the Black children they adopted—and later murdered—untold. Through meticulous and empathetic investigative reporting, Roxanna Asgarian has not just rectified that injustice; she has provided a systemic critique of the predatory, racist child welfare system that is every bit as urgent and undeniable as the movements for police abolition that began in 2020."

—Ethan Brown, *New York Times* bestselling author of *Murder in the Bayou*

"Powerful and urgent, *We Were Once a Family* is a crucial investigation into the deeply flawed system of child 'protection' that forcibly separates families, punishes marginalized communities, perpetuates inequality, and causes generational harm. Through unflinching reporting, immersive prose, and direct testimonies from the families whose children were taken, Roxanna Asgarian's book is a call for justice and systemic change that must be heard."

—Caelainn Hogan, author of *Republic of Shame: How Ireland Punished "Fallen Women" and Their Children*

Roxanna Asgarian

WE WERE ONCE A FAMILY

Roxanna Asgarian is a Texas-based journalist who writes about courts and the law for *The Texas Tribune*. Her work has appeared in *The Washington Post*, *New York* magazine, and *Texas Monthly*, among other publications. She received the 2022 J. Anthony Lukas Work-in-Progress Award for *We Were Once a Family*.

WE WERE ONCE A FAMILY

WE WERE ONCE A FAMILY

A Story of Love, Death, and Child Removal in America

Roxanna Asgarian

Picador
Farrar, Straus and Giroux
New York

Picador

120 Broadway, New York 10271

Library of Congress Control Number: 2022053344

Paperback ISBN: 978-1-250-32192-3

Designed by Patrice Sheridan

Our books may be purchased in bulk for promotional, educational, or
business use. Please contact your local bookseller or the Macmillan
Corporate and Premium Sales Department at 1-800-221-7945,
extension 5442, or by email at MacmillanSpecialMarkets@macmillan.com.

For book club information, please email marketing@picadorusa.com.

picadorusa.com • Follow us on social media at @picador or @picadorusa

D 3 5 7 9 10 8 6 4 2

For my son, Rocco

And in memory of Markis, Hannah, Abigail,
Devonte, Jeremiah, and Ciera

Contents

PART II

Preface

I wrote my first stories about the U.S. foster care system in 2016, while I was working at a city magazine in Houston, Texas. I began by looking deeply at the federal lawsuit against the state for its inhumane treatment of children in long-term foster care. I spent hours and days interviewing people and reading the case file of one of the plaintiffs, Trish Virgil. After being removed from her mother's care because her stepfather had physically and sexually abused her, Trish was bounced around various foster homes and institutions for years before aging out. Once she left care, she ended up right back in the same trailer with her mother and stepfather; she had nowhere else to go. Her story was harrowing, but it was far from unique. In the years since, I have spoken to dozens of young people with lived experience in foster care, and in every single case these folks endured some type of abuse—*after* they entered care.

What we call the "child welfare system" is actually a large web of state, county, and city agencies that each run their own operations, with their own rules and procedures, all with the main goal of protecting children from child abuse and neglect. Because of the sometimes overlapping patchwork of agencies involved, and the fact that most child abuse and neglect cases and adoption cases from foster care are sealed, the child welfare system is a difficult one to report on.

The general understanding of the system, which is responsible for about 425,000 children around the country, is vague at best, and many people hold misconceptions about the parents and children who become entangled within it. Mainstream media outlets often report about the child welfare system only when major cases of child abuse happen; without systemic analysis, these stories can end up promoting more punitive policies aimed at families who need help. In fact, about 75 percent of child welfare cases involve not abuse but neglect, which can often be caused by or confused with poverty.

When reports emerged that two women, a married couple, had crashed their car into the ocean in late March 2018, killing themselves and their six adopted children, I was struck by all the details that were coming out. My friend Shane Dixon Kavanaugh and his team were publishing breaking news stories for *The Oregonian*, Portland's daily newspaper, that revealed long-term abuse by the two white adoptive mothers against their six Black children. Those stories began to paint a sinister picture of the family. When I saw that some of the children came from Harris County, Texas, where I live, I was struck by a gut feeling: I knew that there was much more to this story, and that it started earlier, way earlier, when these kids were still in their homes with their birth parents.

Two weeks after the crash, my phone rang. It was Shane, calling from his office in Portland, and I knew what he was going to say before the words came out of his mouth. Yes, I told him. I can find the kids' birth parents, and I can speak with them.

As a journalist, I was most interested in looking at who has power and who does not—my aim was to write stories that hew closely to the perspective of the people without power, instead of assuming the perspective of those with it. I had done quite a few sensitive interviews by then and had been witness to many people affected by crimes, in the stage when their grief was still shock. Even so, when I first met the Davis family—the relatives of three of the children in the 2018 crash—I was bowled over. This, this felt different. The family's pain ran deep. It was a pain that had existed in their lives since they first lost the children a decade before, and now it was double-edged: they were re-experiencing the trauma of the children's removal, and they were coming to understand that the fantasies they'd told themselves about the lives the children were living were just that, fantasies. The reality was that the children had not been okay. They had not been cared for. They suffered, and then they died. They were murdered.

In the media frenzy over the Hart family tragedy, the deeper story got largely overlooked. While many of the big stories focused on Jennifer and Sarah Hart, stories about the children—who they were, where they came from, what happened to their birth families—were mostly absent. Much of what was written about the kids concentrated only on their harrowing abuse—even as major questions about the child welfare system's role in the deaths went unanswered.

In the coverage of the crash, mainstream media continued in its long-standing tradition of reporting on foster care and adoption almost exclusively through the lens of adoptive parents, while largely leaving out the experiences of adoptees and birth families. We like our adoption stories to be happy endings; many people took note of the Hart case because it contradicted what they thought they knew about adoption. But since there's a scarcity of in-depth reporting about the child welfare system, people zeroed in on the women's motivations and intentions, instead of on the biased decision-making and dehumanizing practices that created the conditions that allowed the Harts' abuse to flourish.

In order for the children's stories to become the book in your hands, the birth families took a huge leap of faith, opening their homes and lives and histories to me, a stranger. I had no personal experience with the foster care system, but I'd had an unstable childhood home life and could relate to some aspects of these families' struggles. Above all, I was struck by the lack of dignity in the way these families were treated, as they repeatedly grieved the loss of their children—first to the state, and then to their murderers.

There is a unique trust that is built between journalist and source over years of spending time and having deep conversations; it's an honor for me to experience that trust.

This is the hardest work I have ever done, and I have routinely confronted the fact that this reporting affected me deeply, even as I knew that the families experiencing this pain firsthand were actually living it each day—pain that is hard to comprehend, that is overwhelming. As journalists, we are often taught to stay stoic, to depersonalize situations, to get out of the way of the story. This ethic has its merits, but it has costs as well.

In this book, I'm not a passive observer of injustice. I note in the text places where I have influenced aspects of the story. I refer to the girlfriend and son of one Davis family member—Dontay—by their nicknames to be considerate of a child who is still a minor. In one case, which is also noted in the text, I have used a pseudonym for another child for the same reason. I used a pseudonym for Tammy's husband, on her request. When Devonte, Jeremiah, and Ciera were adopted by the Harts, the women changed the spelling of Ciera's name to Sierra. I will use the spelling of her name on her original birth certificate throughout.

This book is a culmination of five years of work. The reporting is based on extensive interviews, traveling to key locations, and studying thousands of pages of foster care case files, criminal case records, and law enforcement investigation documents. I conducted the present-day reporting in person unless otherwise noted, and I reconstructed past events by conducting in-depth interviews with multiple sources and examining primary documents related to the events. The work is also informed by my seven years of continuous reporting on the foster care system as a whole.

To investigate the Hart family murder without investigating the role the child welfare system played in it is to ignore the hundreds of thousands of children in foster care around this country, and the physical, sexual, and emotional abuse many of them have experienced while in government care. Telling this story without reporting on the failures of the system is not telling the whole story. By diminishing the children's former lives and sidelining their birth families, the media risks reinforcing the same racist structures and actions that allowed the adoptive parents to hang on to the children after numerous allegations of abuse, the very structures and actions that contributed mightily to these children's deaths. This book, I hope, is a corrective to that.

PART I

Prologue

People come to this place for its sweeping views. Alongside the Pacific Coast Highway, the circular gravel turnoff sits just across from a small bridge over the tiny Juan Creek, and from its edge you can see the rocky Northern California coastline, its cliffs dotted with native grasses and wild succulents. At low tide, you can see the beach where fishermen used to camp, casting their wide nets to catch the night fish that fling themselves onto the waves during spawning season.

A man and his wife were traveling that spring, starting from Alaska and heading down the Pacific Coast Highway, when they parked their RV for the night at that scenic point. It was a spot, halfway between the Oregon border and San Francisco, that showcased the beauty of Northern California, where they could sleep to the sound of the waves crashing below. At about eleven that night, the man heard the sound of a vehicle crunching on the gravel nearby. Being older, the man was careful about where he and his wife bedded down, and he poked his head out to make sure the area was still safe. He saw a big vehicle—not a pickup, but not a sedan either—parked near their RV. Nobody was outside the car. *Seems fine*, he thought, turning in for the night with his wife.

At around three in the morning, he awoke to the sound of tires screeching on gravel, and what sounded like a car bottoming out. He got himself out of bed and left his camper. It was pitch black, and the sound of the waves was steady. No car was in sight. He thought maybe the vehicle that had joined them earlier had peeled out and headed down into town.

He walked to the edge of the cliff. The ocean was a felt presence more than anything; darkness engulfed him. He thought he heard a wail coming from down below. Was it somebody crying for help? He strained his ears, squinting down into the inky blackness. *It must have been a seal*, he thought. He turned back to his camper and rejoined his wife in bed.

The next day, after the couple continued on down the coast, a German tourist stood at the edge of the cliff, looking out at the crashing waves. It was Monday, March 26, 2018, and the sky was clear blue, but something alarming marred her view: at the bottom of the steep and jagged cliff lay an SUV flipped on its roof, crumpled, with the vehicle's undercarriage exposed.

It was about four-thirty in the afternoon on Deputy

Robert Julian's day off when he heard the call about a vehicle in the water. Most of his colleagues were tied up, he knew, two hours down the PCH in Gualala, where a violent altercation between neighbors involving a gun and a shovel left two men in their sixties hospitalized. Julian wasn't doing anything, so he told dispatch he would go.

Dispatch initially told him there was a two-person fatality, and the deputy, who performed coroner duties for the sheriff's office, kept a couple of body bags in his car. But as he was heading out toward the point at Juan Creek where the SUV was found, dispatch told him to be prepared for three more bodies. He stopped by the office and grabbed several more body bags.

By the time he arrived on the scene, it was nearly six o'clock, and emergency vehicles were swarming the turnoff point. A helicopter had just arrived, and firefighters were running from their vehicles to the edge of the cliff. The Westport fire chief filled Julian in: Two people were inside the vehicle, deceased, and three more, apparently children, had been flung from the SUV and were found on the shore. All of them were cold, with rigor mortis. Investigators had found water in the tire well; the usually chilly Pacific Coast ocean water had sat inside long enough to turn warm, indicating the vehicle had been there awhile.

There was a problem, the fire chief told him. The overturned SUV was at the bottom of a steep one-hundred-foot cliff; it would be a major feat to retrieve the vehicle and the bodies inside—it was already clear that the bodies in the driver and front passenger seats couldn't be extricated from the car in its current position. The tow truck that had arrived was not big enough for the job, so they'd sent for a full-size semitruck tower, which was on its way.

In the meantime, Julian grabbed three of the body bags from his trunk and the firefighters descended the cliff to ensconce the three bodies that had been ejected from the car and were on the beach below. The California Highway Patrol helicopter then lifted those bodies to the lookout point, where Julian confirmed they were dead. He found no IDs on the bodies, which he noted were indeed all children.

It was dark by that time, and Julian moved his squad car farther south to another turnoff and directed his brights toward the cliff, to help light the scene below. The industrial tow truck arrived at nearly ten o'clock, and firefighters rappelled down the cliff to attempt to chain the vehicle to the truck. As the SUV—a Yukon—began to lift, a body fell from the driver's seat, smashing against the rocks amid the surf.

The Yukon was lifted to the cliff's edge, and Julian confirmed that the person in the front passenger seat, a blond woman, was deceased. A driver's license found in a tide pool helped him identify her: Sarah Hart. Firefighters retrieved the driver's body from the rocks, putting it in a large lift bucket and using a winch to get it to the cliff. Jennifer Hart's temporary ID was in the glove box of the Yukon, but Julian was unable to identify her—the fall out of the SUV as it was being towed up the cliff had smashed her face so that it was unrecognizable.

As Julian worked on identifying and tagging the bodies,

California Highway Patrol officer Michael Covington and his partner were busy taking down statements from personnel at the scene for the crash report. Over the course of their careers, the officers had responded to dozens of accidents along the Pacific Coast Highway, including vehicles that had crashed down the cliffs, but they noticed something unusual about this one. The turnout had a wide berm, about eighteen inches of raised land along the edge, covered with grass. There were no skid marks anywhere. "It was definitely out of the ordinary," Covington said later, adding that it was "very unusual to have no evidence of any kind to indicate why it went down the cliff."

Back at the office, deputies researched the license plate number to figure out where the deceased came from. They learned that the Harts were a family of eight from Washington—so there were presumably three children still to be found.

The Mendocino County Sheriff's Office search and rescue team hit the beach first thing in the morning. As a volunteer operation, they were able to rustle up eight searchers that Tuesday, but the search was grueling and not very fruitful. A storm had come through just before the crash, and the waves were still choppy. Much of the coastline was inaccessible for all but the most expert searchers, who could rappel down. Jared Chaney, the search team coordinator, said that the shifting tides made for "a whole new beach" every six hours. "You'd search at low tide, you'd find something," he explained. "You'd search at the next high tide, you'd find brand-new things that weren't there when you were there on that very beach the day before."

Drones were dispatched to take detailed videos of the hard-to-reach areas, and each day the number of volunteers crept up. Most were dispatched to the bluffs, asking landowners to allow them access to their properties so that they could use high-powered scopes to search along the coastline. When members of the U.S. Coast Guard assessed the probable locations of the bodies, given the tide pattern and the length of time they'd likely been in the water, they identified a forty-five-mile stretch of coast south of the crash site, from Fort Bragg down to Point Arena. Needing help, the search team put out a call to the surrounding counties.

By the time they'd assembled eighty-five searchers, it was nearing the weekend, and they hadn't yet found any bodies. It wasn't until April 7, nearly two weeks after the crash, that the body of a girl was found on the shore, a mile north of where the SUV had hit the rocks—in the opposite direction of the zone the Coast Guard had predicted. Investigators began working on identification; ten days later, they announced that the body was that of Ciera Hart, age twelve. The three children they'd found on the beach at the time of the crash were Markis Hart, nineteen; Jeremiah Hart, fourteen; and Abigail Hart, also fourteen.

The day after the crash, Mendocino County sheriff Tom Allman had acknowledged at a press conference that there were no skid or brake marks at the spot where the SUV left the cliff, but he hesitated to speculate about the cause. "We have no evidence and no reason to believe this was an intentional act," he told reporters.

Those reporters, and many others around the country, rushed to fill in the details of the family's lives and searched for clues as to what had actually happened. Originally from South Dakota, Jennifer and Sarah, who had been together since college, had adopted one set of three biracial siblings from foster care in Texas in 2006, and a second set of three Black siblings, again from the Texas foster care system, in 2008. They lived with the children first in Alexandria, Minnesota, before moving to West Linn, Oregon (a suburb of Portland), and then to Woodland, Washington, thirty minutes north of Portland.

A breaking news story published the day after the crash by *The Oregonian*, Portland's daily newspaper, detailed how the family had left their Woodland home in a hurry days earlier, after workers from Child Protective Services stopped by to investigate a report of child abuse. Neighbors of the Harts told reporters they'd called CPS after one of the six children, Devonte, age fifteen, had repeatedly come to their house, sometimes late at night, asking for food for himself and his siblings. They said that another sibling, Hannah, sixteen, had once shown up at their door after jumping from a window in her home and told them her mothers were racists and that they were abusing her. But the neighbors didn't report that incident at the time; Jennifer and the rest of the children came to their house the next morning, the neighbors said, and Hannah robotically apologized.

Still, like the Mendocino sheriff, friends of the Harts were hesitant to believe the crash could have been anything but an accident. Zippy Lomax, a good friend of the Harts since 2012, told *The Oregonian*, "Jen and Sarah were the kinds of parents this world desperately needs. They loved their kids more than anything else."

The *Oregonian* story also noted Devonte Hart's presence in a 2014 viral photo that CNN had called "The Hug Shared Around the World": clad in a brown leather jacket, a blue patterned fedora, and blue knit gloves, the then twelve-year-old clutches a police officer; tears are streaming down the boy's face. The photo was taken at a protest against police brutality in Portland after a grand jury in Ferguson, Missouri, declined to indict Officer Darren Wilson for shooting the unarmed eighteen-year-old Michael Brown six times, killing him. Devonte had been standing in front of the police line, holding a sign that said FREE HUGS.

That photo had moved many, but it had also, Lomax told *The Oregonian*, led to the family receiving negative attention for being multiracial and having lesbian parents. Lomax said the family felt hounded by the press and misunderstood by outsiders. "They got a lot of negativity from that, and they kind of closed off for a while, honestly," she explained.

In May 2018, there was finally a breakthrough in the search. A passerby found a pair of pants and a small shoe on the sand in Mendocino, and brought them up to one of the searchers who had been camping on the beach. Closer inspection showed that a decomposed foot was inside the shoe.

The clothes seemed likely to be Hannah's, but initial DNA tests on the remains proved inconclusive.

Devonte Hart, the sibling who received the most national attention, has never been found.

In the early days after the crash, the media presented no information at all about the birth families of the children. Part of the reason for the silence was logistical: Child welfare cases are largely sealed. The adoption agency used by the Harts, which had a history of violations, was now defunct, and former employees weren't talking. And Texas, where the children were born, wouldn't even share the names of the birth family members with the police investigating the crime. As is often the case, reporters went where the trail led them, focusing on publicly available records and recollections from friends, family members, and neighbors of the Harts.

Jennifer Hart was a heavy Facebook user whose posts about her family were verbose and always accompanied by well-lit photos of the kids, constantly smiling. Predictably, the media frenzy over the Hart family tragedy emphasized the contrast between Jennifer's public image and her true intentions and psychological motivations. Stories about the children—who they were, where they came from, what happened to their birth families—were virtually absent. Much of what was written about the kids focused only on their harrowing abuse. And above all, the major question—*How could this have happened?*—went unanswered.

1

"Every Time I See You, You Take Me Away"

It was a mild December day in Houston, and Dontay Davis had started a fight at school again. His cousin Boogie found him in the halls of the Gregory-Lincoln Education Center, the Fourth Ward school both boys attended. It was 2006 and Dontay was in fifth grade. Boogie was a couple of years older, but he'd flunked a grade and so was just one year ahead.

Dontay had always been a fighter. Sometimes fights started when a kid would say something to him he didn't like, but other times he'd pick them himself. He wanted to show the others in his school that he wasn't a punk, and he told himself that's why he did it, but really, deep down, he liked the way it felt to exchange punches, even when he lost. It released something in him he was always carrying; for a moment, he felt clear and light. The fight that day, he remembers, had been with another boy over a girl in class. So when Dontay met up with Boogie in the hallways at school, he expected his cousin to talk about that. Instead, Boogie asked him if he knew what was going on at his house.

The lightness vanished and a pit landed in Dontay's stomach as he heard the words come out of his cousin's mouth. Before Boogie had even told him what was happening, he knew that it was Child Protective Services, and he knew he was going to have to leave.

During class later, Dontay got called to the office. His CPS caseworker, Tamika Lipsey, was waiting for him. He asked her point-blank if she was going to take him away.

"Why do you always ask me that?" she said.

He didn't trust her, because he knew what happened when the caseworker showed up. "Every time I see you, you take me away," he told her.

Tamika assured him that she was only there to visit with him and make sure he was okay. He relaxed a bit, but she still asked him the same questions she always asked, questions he felt uncomfortable answering because he was always afraid of saying the wrong thing and he didn't want to get his family in trouble. He knew what would happen if they got in trouble—he'd have to leave again, and maybe get split up from his brothers and baby sister again, and if he ended up back at the shelter he'd have to fight the big kids again to prove to the others that they shouldn't fuck with him, and those kids were not like the kids at Gregory-Lincoln. They were meaner, and they were bigger. And worse, he knew he wouldn't be able to see his mom, Sherry, anymore, and the family had only just got back to some sort of normal.

Tamika asked him how he liked living at his aunt's house, where he'd been staying with his siblings for close to six months. He told her he liked it—he got to play with his brothers Devonte and Jeremiah, with his cousins in the Fourth Ward neighborhood where his mother grew up, and on the computer at his aunt's house. She asked him if there was anything he didn't like, and he was careful to say no. She asked him what happened when he got in trouble. He told her he got spankings on his butt from his aunt; he hoped that was the right thing to say. He told his caseworker that on some weekends, they'd go back to Nathaniel Davis's house, where they last lived before they were taken into foster care, and Nathaniel, whom Dontay referred to as his dad, would cook for them and they'd sleep over.

Tamika left Dontay there at school and went back to the CPS office. She didn't tell him this, but she had been disconcerted by her visit earlier that day to the apartment where Dontay lived with his two younger brothers and baby sister. Before she had gone to see Dontay at his school, she'd gone to check in with his aunt Priscilla Celestine. Priscilla's brother Clarence was the father of Dontay's two youngest siblings, Jeremiah and Ciera, and he had asked her to take the children in when they were removed from their home.

Priscilla was a churchgoing woman, unlike her brother, who was in prison for drugs, and her brother's girlfriend, Sherry, Dontay's mom, who had a well-known cocaine problem that had caused her to lose her children. Priscilla worked as a receptionist at a hospital and kept her nose clean—Dontay had told his caseworker, when she asked if they went to church, "That's the only place we ever go."

But Priscilla had been struggling with the new family setup, which had formed abruptly months after the kids were taken away from their home. The children had been in foster care at separate placements before they moved in with her. She was growing to love the children, especially her brother's two, who were the youngest. And she wanted to keep all the siblings together—but four more children in her home, when it used to be just her and her daughter and granddaughter, strained her patience at times.

More than that, it strained her resources. This was 2006, more than a decade before Texas's Department of Family and Protective Services began issuing a monthly payment of $350 for each child who was placed with relatives. Foster parents had long been given monthly stipends on a sliding scale to care for children, with high-needs children drawing the most money. But kinship placements, in which children were placed with relatives, didn't qualify for those payments; instead, caregivers received a one-time $1,000 payment for the first child and $495 for each sibling, along with $500 a year for approved expenses.

For Priscilla's family of seven, it just wasn't enough, between new beds for the four children, increased grocery bills, clothes and shoes, school supplies, and diapers. The financial strain was exacerbated by the fact that Priscilla, whose two-bedroom apartment did not pass a home inspection because it was too small to accommodate the entire family, had needed to upgrade to a larger, four-bedroom unit in order for the children to be able to stay with her for the long term.

She needed her full-time job more than ever, but there was also the matter of finding people to care for the children when she was at work. Dontay, ten years old, was in school, but the younger ones weren't—Devonte was four, Jeremiah was two, and Ciera had just turned a year old when they moved in. She enlisted her daughter as the chief caretaker when she was away, but sometimes her daughter was busy. And Dontay's school had been repeatedly calling her to come in, since he was always picking fights and getting into trouble. She needed to keep her job to have a chance in hell of paying for the kids, but she wasn't sure she would be able to handle the new situation without help.

She'd regularly send the kids to their father figure, Nathaniel Davis—he wasn't the biological dad of any of the kids, but he had given his last name to all of them. Nathaniel was the much-older partner of Sherry, the kids' mom. They'd been together for a long time, and even though she was in and out of relationships with other men, he thought of her as his wife and thought of her children as his own. In fact, he'd been the primary parent caring for them since they were born. When Priscilla called, Nathaniel was over the moon to help. He had missed his children terribly since they'd been taken from his home the year before, after Sherry failed a drug test for the second time upon the birth of Ciera. He was hopeful that one day, after all the drama had quieted down, the kids would return to live with him.

And that wasn't the only support Priscilla had. Sherry was keen to stay involved in her children's lives. Priscilla had had to call and bother the caseworker multiple times about a clothing stipend for the children, who had badly needed winter clothes. But when Sherry came to visit she brought them the coolest new Nike sneakers and Polo shirts and Tommy Hilfiger jeans, even for the babies, as well as bags full of McDonald's to fill the kids' bellies. Sherry told Priscilla that if she ever needed her to watch the kids, she was only a call away. She missed her children, and although she wasn't able to stay clean, she wanted nothing more than to be in their lives.

The problem was, Sherry had terminated her parental rights—her lawyer had said it was necessary to do so in order for Priscilla to be able to adopt them. This meant that she was no longer supposed to have contact with them at all. It was a condition of the children living with Priscilla that Sherry never be left alone with them. And Priscilla knew she shouldn't risk it.

But there were times when there really were no better options. And one of those times was the very day Tamika Lipsey visited Dontay at Gregory-Lincoln and told him she wasn't going to take him away. Before she went to Dontay's school, Tamika had stopped by Priscilla's apartment unannounced and found a strange woman in pajamas at the door.

She said her name was Sherry, and that she was a "family friend." Concerned, Tamika asked Sherry if she lived there. She said no, she just spent the night because Priscilla had to be at work early. The kids looked like they had just woken up, and when Tamika went to check their rooms she noticed none of them had any furniture. Sherry explained that the family had only moved into the apartment a couple of weeks before, and showed her which rooms were for which children.

Tamika called her supervisor once she'd arrived back at the office after checking on Dontay at school. Her supervisor told her to remove the kids, based on the potential risk of harm.

Sherry Davis was a Black woman from the Fourth Ward in Houston, Texas. Historically the center of Black life in Houston, the neighborhood was once known as the Mother Ward; before that, it was called Freedmen's Town. It was where formerly enslaved people from the plantations along the Brazos River settled after news of the Confederacy's defeat finally reached Galveston and the enslaved people in Texas came to know that they were free.

These newly freed people had settled on the marshy, flood-prone banks of Buffalo Bayou, along the same sludgy river that the brothers Augustus and John Allen had traversed in 1836 when they founded what would become Houston. At the time the freedmen settled the Fourth Ward in the late 1860s, the city didn't exist much beyond downtown, and the banks of the bayou were considered undesirable property. It was here that the freedmen made and laid their own red-brick roads, carving symbols of hope on each one, and set to building homes and churches for the free Black families.

The Fourth Ward's story is similar to that of many other freedmen's towns around the country: In 1950, as cars became widely accessible, the government constructed an interstate highway, ramming it through the ward, and the community, cut in half, began to atrophy. Integration meant that well-to-do Black families, of which there were many in the Fourth Ward, began to settle in suburbs outside the city's core. The Black community shrank, and those who remained were very poor. In the 1980s, crack cocaine took a firm hold. Then, after decades when the local real estate held barely any monetary value, the neighborhood, next door to downtown, suddenly became hot. Developers bought much of the land, sometimes by force, and renamed a good chunk of it Midtown, redefining its identity and erecting manicured retail centers filled with smoothie shops and chain pizzerias.

Sherry was born in 1970, by which time the Fourth Ward was already in decline. She and her younger siblings, Joshua and Alisia, lived with their mother in a white shotgun house with a gabled roof on the corner of Ruthven and Matthews, three blocks down from Mount Carmel Missionary Baptist Church. Sherry's mother, Rose Mary Harlan, had herself grown up in the Fourth Ward, and Rose's sister Doris lived across the street.

Rose lived with her boyfriend, Lonnie Ray Curtis. Lonnie used to hit Rose in front of her children. He brandished his pistol, the children remembered, pointing it at her at least once and beating her so hard with it another time that she ended up in the hospital. One night, when Sherry was twelve, she was sleeping in a bedroom of the little shack with her younger siblings, who were eleven and eight, and Lonnie's five-year-old, when Lonnie came home drunk. Sherry and her sister, Alisia, were awake, and heard their mother arguing with Lonnie about where he had been.

Rose pointed out Lonnie's messed-up hair, accused him of philandering, and told him to sleep on the couch. That's when Sherry and Alisia heard Lonnie rummaging around in the cabinet in their mother's room. Shortly after that, they heard a gunshot.

The girls fled their room and found their mother stumbling out of her bedroom with blood spurting out of her neck.

"Rose, please don't die," Lonnie pleaded with her. "Come lay down on the bed."

Sherry saw her mother hit the floor, collapsing in the doorway with her head twisted at an unnatural angle, framed by the edge of the doorframe. Lonnie grabbed the .22, put it in his pocket, and fled across the street to wake up Rose's sister Doris.

Rose was dead by the time the ambulance arrived, and Lonnie, at twenty-four, was charged with her murder. Sherry and her siblings went at first to live with their aunt but often moved around, even, at times, sleeping in cars. It was while on the street that Sherry was introduced to crack cocaine, which would come to shape her life.

At fifteen years old, just three years after her mother's murder, Sherry became mother to a son, DeMarcus. Her second son, DeAndre, came shortly after. She dropped out of high school and took up with an abusive boyfriend, who controlled her movements. She left DeMarcus and DeAndre with a friend, and after the friend didn't hear from her for a couple weeks, they called CPS. Sherry said her boyfriend had kidnapped her and wouldn't let her leave his house; she lost the boys, who were adopted out of foster care.

Sherry was pregnant with her third son when she reconnected with Nathaniel Davis. She'd known him for most of her life; he went by Joe Boy, and he grew up across the street from her mom and aunts back in the day. He was much older—when they reconnected, Sherry was nineteen and Nathaniel was forty-seven; he had been married and divorced, and had grown children. He was steady, though. He did yard work and was staying with his mom while he got his disability benefits together, and once he did that, he was going to get a place of his own.

Sherry moved into that place with him, along with her new son, baby DeQuince. The nature of their relationship was unusual: Nathaniel and Sherry had a partnership that would last decades, but she repeatedly had dalliances and sometimes serious relationships outside of their pairing. Nathaniel never fathered any of Sherry's children. He did raise and nurture them all, though. He knew that he hadn't done it right with his own kids the first time—he wasn't around enough for them, and his one grown biological son wouldn't talk to him because of it—and he wanted to do right by Sherry's children. He wanted to be a good father.

When DeQuince was three months old, his biological dad stopped by and asked Nathaniel if he could take him out. When he returned, DeQuince's arm was sore and swollen. His biological father told Sherry he'd fallen out of his stroller at the park. But when Nathaniel took him into Ben Taub, the public hospital downtown, they told him DeQuince had multiple broken bones. Crazed, Sherry came to the hospital and took DeQuince home, terrified that CPS workers would take him as they had taken her other children.

And, of course, they did. Nathaniel wanted to fight CPS to get DeQuince back, but Sherry wouldn't do it. Instead, she began to use more crack cocaine, tipping her cigarettes with the white powder before smoking them. Shortly after DeQuince went to live with a woman in Sunnyside, another poor Black Houston neighborhood, he was adopted, too.

When Dontay was born to a man Sherry was not in a serious relationship with, she gave the newborn Nathaniel's last name, Davis, and the family left the Fourth Ward and settled down near Sunnyside. Sherry worked as a home health aide, leaving for several days at a time to stay in the home of the elderly patients she cared for, and she prided herself on not needing welfare checks to get by.

Dontay was five years old when Devonte was born, and Dontay loved being a big brother. Nathaniel would cook for the boys and clean up after them, and take Devonte to the hospital when his asthma got bad. By all accounts Sherry loved her kids—she kept her boys fed and clothed in fresh new sneakers. But she still had her cocaine habit. She'd get stressed and reach for her pack of cigarettes, slap them against her hand to pack them down, and sprinkle the white powder in the space left at the top. Lighting her primos, as she called them, made her feel good and helped her forget about the drama of the day.

Sherry took up with a new man, Clarence, but the kids stayed with Nathaniel, whom they considered their father.

Nathaniel told people he and Sherry were still together, and they were, in a way—whenever she came to stay, she cooked for her children and cleaned up around the house, and he raised the children when she was out. She'd stay out for days, sometimes for her job but other times for other reasons.

When Jeremiah was born in 2004, Sherry and the baby tested positive for cocaine, and Nathaniel got custody of the children, which really just solidified the relationship they already had in place. The boys got a bunk bed, and Jeremiah's new crib was rolled in. Nathaniel's grown daughter Carmenel came most days to help with the baby, and the boys slept in Nathaniel's bed, all piled in together, while the new bunk bed sat empty in the boys' room.

Dontay, Devonte, and baby Jeremiah were Nathaniel's whole life, and he told the CPS caseworker that if he had to choose between Sherry and the children, he'd keep his kids in a heartbeat.

The situation was stable but still tenuous, with the threat of removal always hanging over the family. Because of Sherry's history with the agency, and especially because of the abuse of DeQuince, caseworkers kept a close eye on the Davis family.

In 2005, Sherry gave birth to a baby girl she named Ciera. Sherry was still with Clarence Celestine, who was also Jeremiah's father. In the hospital, Sherry again tested positive for cocaine, although the baby tested negative. She pleaded with the caseworkers, asking them to give her another chance. But her child welfare case was moved from the "reunification" track to the "termination" track, and the kids were taken from Nathaniel's house, in part because he told them he didn't know Sherry was using again. He had meant that she was never high around the kids, which is when he spent time with her, but they had seen his response as "enabling" her drug use.

The four kids were first sent to Nathaniel's brother's house, but after a caseworker stopped by and found the brother and his wife drunk, baby Ciera was sent to one foster family and the boys were moved to another. Eight-year-old Dontay lasted less than two weeks at the home, where he noticed there was a dog gate erected in the living room, separating the foster children from the foster parents' biological children. The boys' meals were strictly portioned, while the couple's children got to eat what they liked. Dontay became enraged—he was old enough to understand they'd taken him from his family but not old enough to understand why.

The foster mother reported to his caseworker that when he would get angry, his eyes would roll back in his head and he would threaten his siblings and the other children in the home. The caseworker dropped him off at the CPS offices, and as she left, Dontay told her he was going to set her on fire for taking him there.

Dontay was sent to Intracare, one of Houston's few psychiatric hospitals that accepted Medicaid patients. Intracare was at one time the second-largest psychiatric hospital in Harris County, before it was shut down in 2012 after the Centers for Medicare and Medicaid terminated its contract with the hospital for improper use of restraints and seclusion, a practice that posed a danger to patient health. Twice, the hospital was cited for chemically restraining patients without an updated treatment plan. Here, Dontay received a diagnosis of oppositional defiant disorder. Later, he'd be diagnosed with ADHD and bipolar disorder as well.

Dontay spent three weeks at Intracare in 2005, and he saw children there who were like him, children whose emotions were too much for them to handle. It was scary—there was the constant threat of a sedative shot, administered into the flesh of the butt, that would make you fall unconscious. He saw others get the shot, which they called "booty juice," and he got it, too—more times than he could count.

But people were real in there, he thought. They didn't pretend that everything was okay, that strangers were family, or that they cared and wanted to help. For the first time since he'd left his family, he felt like people were being honest.

Dontay bounced from the hospital to an emergency shelter to another foster placement before he finally got to reunite with his siblings at their aunt Priscilla's house in the summer of 2006. That year, almost 348,000 children in Texas had been the subject of child welfare investigations, and 32,000 of those children were in the care of the state.

In 2004, the state comptroller, Carole Keeton Strayhorn, released a scathing report titled "Forgotten Children," detailing high caseloads of up to thirty-five children per caseworker; this figure, more than double the recommended amount, resulted in nearly a quarter of the state's caseworkers vacating their jobs each year. The report found that kids were often moved around from place to place and that some hadn't seen their caseworker in months. It also showed photographic evidence of the squalor some foster children were living in, with some attending "therapeutic camps" where they had to use primitive outhouses and cook their own food outside, using meat patties that had been packed in coolers with no ice. "I challenge any defender of the status quo to put their child or grandchild in some of the places I've seen for one day, much less for a lifetime," Keeton Strayhorn wrote in a statement issued after her report.

In 2005, the Texas legislature passed a reform bill that aimed to address some of the failures of its child welfare system by reorganizing the Department of Family and Protective Services. The bill would fully privatize its placement services and add $250 million to DFPS's budget to hire 3,200 more caseworkers. But the move backfired, in a sense—from 2004 to 2006, the number of children removed from their homes increased from about 13,500 to about 17,500. The state had increased funding for CPS investigations but did not allocate additional funding for the foster placements—or for preventive services, like drug treatment and parenting classes, aimed at keeping kids in their homes.

With placements at capacity, CPS acknowledged that children had been sleeping in their offices, with nowhere else to go. The privatization of placements was no remedy and had its own complications. In 2006, when Dontay and his siblings were reunited at their aunt's house, three children had died in foster care in different Fort Worth–area homes; they had all been placed by the same private agency, Mesa Family Services. The fallout stalled the state's desired goal of putting its child welfare system, including both placement services and case management, fully in the hands of private providers.

Instead, the agency was in limbo, responsible for more children than ever before but with a lack of quality placements to house them. Caseworkers were given far too many children to look after, and, because of that, the best interests of each individual child were subordinated to other concerns—such as the need to check all the boxes and stay out of the news for high-profile failures resulting in deaths of children.

But Dontay didn't know about any of this. All he knew was that when the caseworker came around, he was in danger of being taken from his family. It had happened before, and he had lived every day with a pit in his stomach, waiting for it to happen again.

That mild December day, his caseworker, Tamika Lipsey, assured him at school that she was just checking up on him, but when he walked up to his apartment after school, she was there again, in front of the apartment, putting his siblings into her car. His mom was standing out there, too, crying, begging Tamika to reconsider.

When Tamika had gotten the go-ahead from her supervisor, she'd driven back to the apartment from the office and found Sherry still there with the three youngest children. She ordered Sherry to dress them, and she told the children to kiss their mother. The children weren't sure what was happening, but they knew their mom was upset, so they started to cry.

Unlike his siblings, Dontay understood in a split second

what was going on. He began to cry, too, and hugged his mother. He told her he would be back; she said, "I hope." She kissed him on the cheek and told him to look after his brothers and sister.

In the car, Dontay took Devonte's face into his hands. The four-year-old Devonte was quiet, observant—he always seemed to the rest of the family to be wiser than his years. Dontay told his brother, "I love you. This ain't nothing . . . I'll always be there."

Dontay ended up in one foster home, and his siblings went to another. The pit in his stomach spread to his whole body. His biggest fear had come true, and he had a feeling deep down that this time the separation was for good. He knew his mom's phone number, and as soon as he could, he snuck to the phone in his foster home without his foster mom seeing him. During that phone call, his mom promised him that she was doing everything she could to get them back. "Be calm," she told him.

But Dontay wasn't calm. He was sure he would never see his siblings again—and when he had strong feelings like that, he knew they would come true. It was nearly Christmas, and Dontay wanted to be home. He didn't get to open all his presents from his aunt, and nobody knew him at the place he was staying. He tried his mother again on the phone, but she didn't pick up.

Dontay, still just ten years old, took his belt, tightened it around his neck, and tied it to the bedpost. "I felt hopeless," he says more than a decade later about that time in his life. "Ain't nothing to live for."

2

A Safe Place

On January 8, 2007, Tamika Lipsey, Dontay's caseworker, picked him up from West Oaks Hospital, where he had spent Christmas heavily sedated. It was the first time she'd seen him since he'd attempted suicide weeks before.

Dontay immediately asked Tamika where his Christmas presents were. "I gave him the presents from the agency," Tamika wrote in her case notes. "He appeared disappointed." Dontay asked her about the video game his aunt had promised to buy him; she told him she would follow up with his aunt to see if she had it. (She never did.)

Tamika asked Dontay what was going on "at the time the suicide incident occurred." He told her he didn't want to be at the foster home anymore. "I made him promise that next time he is going through something like that he needs to call me and if I am not there, give me the opportunity to call him back," she wrote in her notes.

Tamika told Dontay that until he was more stable he'd be going to live at Serenity Place, a residential treatment center in North Houston for youth with behavior problems. His case was designated as "specialized," unlike those of his brothers and sister, who were considered at "basic" level. RTCs took only specialized kids, who required more supervision and brought in more money each day from the state than kids with lower-level designations did.

Dontay had been started on this path the moment he split from his siblings the first time, and now the chasm between them was firmly set: children have to earn their way out of RTCs by showing that their behavior has improved enough to satisfy the facility's requirements. But the facilities themselves are more like jails than loving homes, which doesn't always motivate children to be better behaved. "I told him our goal was to try to channel his anger into more positive outlets," Tamika wrote.

While Dontay was settling in at Serenity Place, Devonte, Jeremiah, and Ciera were being moved into yet another foster home. The foster parents at the home they'd gone to after being removed from their aunt Priscilla's apartment had refused to transport them to visits with Dontay. "The agency made every attempt to compromise with the foster parents," Tamika wrote, "but they stated they were not going to do it."

At the end of January, the siblings were all able to meet for the first time in more than a month. Priscilla was also allowed to visit, along with her daughter and granddaughter. She'd called to ask if Nathaniel could come as well, but after checking with her supervisor, the caseworker said no.

When Priscilla arrived at the CPS office, what she didn't know at first was that she was there to say goodbye to the kids—forever. As soon as she understood what was happening, she asked Tamika if she'd be able to get them back. She was told, flatly, no—she'd have no contact with the children after that day. Priscilla started to cry. "I wish you would have told me that *after* the visit," she told them. She'd brought toys for the children, and they took photos. In one, Priscilla smiled while holding Ciera in her lap. Ciera, clad in a pink shirt and skirt with pastel-toned sneakers, clutched a Barbie doll in one hand and draped the other comfortably over her aunt's arm. In another, Jeremiah and Devonte looked up for the flash as they played with trucks.

Back in August 2006, when Priscilla first got the children, she'd hired Shonda Jones, a family law attorney, to help her adopt them. Shonda advised Sherry and Clarence to voluntarily terminate their rights, which was a necessary step, she said, to free the children for Priscilla to adopt. Sherry and Clarence's parental rights, as well as the rights of Dontay's and Devonte's fathers, who were unknown to the court, were terminated on August 29, 2006.

"She said if we gave our rights up, Priscilla would have a better chance," Clarence said of his decision. What Clarence didn't realize was that once his and Sherry's rights were terminated, the children would be free for adoption not just by Priscilla, but by any interested party. That's because many caseworkers around the country consider the federally

mandated preference to place children with their relatives
to be null once those children are legally severed from their
parents.

Sherry Davis said she felt pressured to relinquish her
rights in order for the state to give her children to Priscilla.
But if she hadn't voluntarily relinquished her rights, Texas
would almost definitely have moved to terminate them. In
1997, Congress passed the Adoption and Safe Families Act
in response to the problem of children remaining in foster
care for long periods. ASFA triggers a timeline the moment
a child welfare case is initiated in the courts—if a child has
been in foster care for fifteen of the last twenty-two months,
states are required to file for termination of parental rights,
thus allowing possible adoptions to occur. The law aimed to
correct what was perceived at the time as a pressing problem:
children's rights to permanent homes were taking a back seat
to the desires and wishes of biological parents, who, critics
said, should not be given years to try to win their children
back. Since ASFA was passed, many states have approved
their own legislation to comport with it, often setting even
shorter timelines to termination. In Texas, the routine is especially streamlined: caseworkers file for possible termination alongside a separate reunification plan the moment a
child is removed from their home.

The explicit goal of ASFA was to reduce the amount of
time kids spent in foster care by cutting the time it took to
free them up for adoption into "permanent, stable homes,"
as Representative Deborah Pryce, an Ohio Republican, told

legislators during the debate over the bill. Pryce and others made clear that they considered children's rights to a safe and stable home largely in opposition to the rights of their parents. "Too often a foster child's best interest, along with common sense, are abandoned as courts and welfare agencies work overtime to put children back in dangerous situations in the name of family reunification," Pryce said. "Let us do it for the children."

Even though the law calls for giving a preference to placing children with relatives over nonrelatives, the "permanent, stable" homes that politicians envisioned were clearly adoptive homes. "Terminating parental rights is the critical first step in moving children into permanent placements," Republican senator John Chafee of Rhode Island argued at the time.

ASFA is seen as one of the most consequential pieces of child welfare legislation in recent history. More than one million children have been adopted from foster care since its passage. At the same time, ASFA helped create a wave of more than two million children whose parents' rights have been terminated—and Black children are 2.4 times more likely to have their parents' rights terminated than are white children. Today, there are fewer children spending years in foster care than before the law passed, the main goal of the legislation. And yet thousands are still legally disconnected from their biological family each year with no assurance of being adopted or finding any other type of permanent home. As a result, about twenty thousand youth in foster care "age out" of the foster care system each year without ever finding a permanent home—that's more than 400,000 young people since ASFA became law, according to the latest data.

Despite being told she would never see the children again, Priscilla wasn't ready to give up. After she left that final visit, she again called her lawyer, Shonda Jones. The family pooled together several thousand dollars, and in May 2007, Priscilla filed a petition to terminate the state's rights to the children and to formally adopt them herself. She didn't know that the children had already been placed on the Texas Adoption Resource Exchange, a public website where interested parties can search for a child who meets their specifications, including race, gender, age, disability status, and whether the child is part of a sibling group.

As the case wound through the courts, the three youngest Davis children were placed in a home that was strict, even by the caseworker's standards. By this time, their caseworker Tamika Lipsey had been replaced by Monica Ajasin, who reported that the foster mother was "constantly redirecting" the kids, who at that time were four, three, and two. "She wants them to sit in a certain way and watch TV like adults and not move their body or even express any view or emotion about what they are watching," Monica wrote in the case file. "I told her that she needs to calm down and give positive reinforcement and should not always nick pick [*sic*] on their shortcomings. I told her that they are children and certain behavior is expected of them."

The foster mother had a litany of complaints against the children: Devonte would try to remove his seat belt while she was driving the car, and took food and snacks from his siblings. Jeremiah, the foster mother noted, would wet the bed and "dig at [his] private parts" and other parts of his body. Ciera "screams and cries for anything," she told the caseworker. She couldn't understand any of them, she said, and Devonte "rattles on and on."

"I asked the [foster mother] if there is anything positive about this [sic] children because all she has said is everything negative," Monica wrote in July 2007.

As for Dontay, the oldest, he had been acting out violently at Serenity Place, the RTC. Incident reports detailed kicking, hitting, and punching, as well as banging his head when frustrated. He was restrained by staff multiple times in what he described as "the control position"—stomach on the floor, ankles crossed, and arms by his sides, with his chin on the floor. "He said that they are punished to lay like that for 10 minutes and afterwards he is calm," his case file notes. His service level was raised from "specialized" to "intense," a DFPS signifier that means a child's behaviors "present an imminent and critical danger of harm to self or others." The designation raised the daily rate that the RTC received from $46.25 to $82.22, and sealed Dontay's fate for the foreseeable future. When Dontay asked about getting to go back with his siblings, his caseworker told him that unless his behavior changed significantly, he would have no chance at going to a less restrictive foster home—and that even if he did improve, he wouldn't be moving back in with his siblings, because the foster home they were living in couldn't accommodate any more children.

The next reported sibling visit didn't occur until August 2007, seven months after Dontay and his siblings last saw each other. At that visit, Dontay had a "flat affect" and played by himself with the toys at the office. "There was no signs of bonding between him and his younger siblings," the caseworker wrote. At the time, Dontay was on a litany of medications, which included the antipsychotic Risperdal; an anticonvulsant called Depakote, used to treat bipolar disorder; two ADHD medications, Adderall and Tenex; and Cogentin, an anti-tremor medication typically given to people with Parkinson's that in Dontay's case was used to offset the combined side effects of all the other drugs.

At the next sibling visit, in late November, the caseworker noted that he seemed to be "drugged up." When she asked the Serenity Place staff member who escorted Dontay to the CPS office about this, he told her, "I don't know. I'm only transporting him to the visit."

Meanwhile, Priscilla's bid for the children was not going as the family had planned. Nathaniel contributed financially, but he felt sidelined in the process. He didn't understand why the kids had been removed from him in the first place—he never touched drugs or even alcohol; the kids had their own room, and they were getting by on his disability benefits. "I should have had those children," he said. "They belonged with me."

Nathaniel continued to try to visit Dontay, although caseworkers would not allow it, as he wasn't the legal parent. He'd drop off CDs and clothes to the CPS office; the caseworker would make note of the gifts in her file, but Dontay never received them. Christmases without any family at all were especially hard. "Everybody else would get visits with their family, and presents, and I never had anyone," Dontay says.

Shonda Jones's thinking was that Priscilla would look good in the eyes of the court. With her pristine lack of criminal history, her churchgoing ways, her steady full-time job, and her lack of real connection to Sherry, she offered the best chance of reuniting the children with their family. "I really felt Priscilla was a safe place," Shonda said.

The case was assigned to the 313th District Court, one of the three courts in Harris County dedicated to CPS and juvenile justice cases. The court rejected Priscilla's bid for adoption, partly because, according to state law, children must stay in a prospective adoptive home for six months before an adoption can be finalized. Even though that requirement can be waived, the judge chose not to do so. The Davis kids had spent five and a half months with Priscilla, two weeks shy of the requirement.

In October 2008, Priscilla appealed the court's decision, but the family had no real idea of what was going on with the children. They'd heard through Shonda that the kids were now living out of state, maybe in Wisconsin, and that a white family wanted to adopt them. But because the adoption process is sealed, the family couldn't find out any details at all. During Priscilla's adoption attempt, Shonda filed a discovery request in court seeking answers for some basic questions about the other potential adoptive family: What were their names? How old were they? What did they do for a living? Were there other children living in the home? Shonda asked for the types of reports, studies, and/or investigations that the potential adoptive parents were subject to, and asked to know whether they were involved in any criminal investigations. To all these questions, DFPS responded, "The information requested is confidential."

In fact, by Christmas 2007, the three youngest children had piqued the interest of a family in Minnesota. The Interstate Compact on the Placement of Children went into effect for the Davis children, triggering a home study of the prospective adoptive family's home and a background check. Meanwhile, the kids' caseworker told the foster mother to begin prepping them for their move. The foster mother said she thought Devonte, the oldest of the three, would "understand a little bit," and the caseworker told her the adoptive parents would be coming to visit the children once the ICPC review went through.

In June 2008, the kids were sent to live with the Minnesota couple, and by the next January, Devonte, Jeremiah, and Ciera were formally adopted. It wasn't until July 15, 2010— more than a year after the adoption was finalized—that Texas's First District Court of Appeals affirmed the decision of the lower court against Priscilla, effectively closing the case and dashing her hopes.

A former Harris County judge in CPS cases, Michael Schneider, was not involved in the Davis children's case, but he reviewed the case details years later. Schneider said that the children's adoption should have been put on hold as

Priscilla's appeal went through the courts; if the appeal had been successful, the children's adoption would have been void. "Somebody dropped the ball," he said.

The family gave up, hoping that one day the children would get back in touch with them. Priscilla tucked away her grief, like she'd done many times throughout her life. "When they took them away, I prayed and thought it must be God's will, and they must be in a better place," Priscilla said, more than ten years later, inside her apartment at the same public housing complex where she had lived with the children. "I told myself that."

A week before Devonte, Jeremiah, and Ciera were to board the plane to start a new life in Minnesota, their older brother Dontay asked his caseworker if he could have a home visit with his siblings. He hadn't stopped asking after them. He proposed they go on an outing together. "Dontay would brighten up when he asked questions but would look blank and sad when I answered," the caseworker wrote.

Nobody had told Dontay that his siblings were likely going to be adopted, or that they were moving out of state in a week. He didn't know that he would never be able to reunite with them, that there was no chance he'd be placed back with them, and that these decisions were final. If he asked questions about his siblings, his mom, or his aunt—such as when he'd be able to see them again—his caseworker told him to ask his therapist. But Dontay didn't trust his therapist—he didn't trust anyone he associated with CPS.

"They'd ask me what's going on with me, and I'd say, 'I got my problems and you got your problems,'" Dontay says now. "By me telling you what's going on with me, how are you helping me? You're not getting me home."

June 11, 2008, arrived; Dontay, by then eleven years old, sat alone at the CPS office, waiting for a scheduled visit with his siblings. It's not clear why, but no one showed up that day. His siblings left Texas two days later. He never got to say goodbye. He didn't even know they were leaving.

3

The Good Ol' Boys Club

If you want to understand the Davis family's case, and how it was fast-tracked into an adoption proceeding while a legal challenge was still under way on behalf of the children's birth family, it's important to understand the court that made the decision. The case, like those of thousands of other families in Harris County, initially landed in the 313th District Court, which was overseen for more than fifteen years by Patrick Shelton, a big, burly man known for his unorthodox courtroom antics. When Shelton took the bench back in 1994, it was the beginning of a new way of running things in the three courts that were responsible for hearing juvenile and CPS cases in Harris County. Under his direction, speed was prioritized and many biological families felt they got short shrift.

Shelton hails from the small West Texas town of Kermit, but he grew up in a West Houston suburb called Spring

Branch, which, like much of central and south central Texas, was settled by German immigrants in the 1800s. It remained largely unincorporated farmland until the 1950s, when the national housing boom hit Houston and its signature sprawl began to take shape. Several wealthy areas near Spring Branch incorporated into what's now known as the Memorial Villages, which are six distinct and pricey municipalities with their own fire and police departments. Spring Branch itself was largely annexed by Houston, although the mostly white neighborhood maintained its small-town atmosphere through Shelton's teen years.

At Spring Woods High School, from which he graduated in 1970, Shelton played football with a fellow classmate, John Phillips, who would go on to serve alongside Shelton as a prosecutor in the Harris County District Attorney's Office in the '80s. By that time, the pair's hometown was seeing large apartment complexes pop up, and some old residents didn't take kindly to the new diversity. As Central American and Korean immigrants began to move in and set up shops and restaurants, white residents became vocal in their opposition to what they saw as the degrading of their neighborhood, which sat near some of the most exclusive suburbs of Houston. In the early '80s, a proposed public housing project only got as far as a fence and a sign, which residents repeatedly spray-painted with the words "No Niggers."

Shelton was hired as a prosecutor under DA John Holmes Jr., who helmed the office for twenty-one years and in that time sentenced more than two hundred people to death, giving Harris County the nickname "Death Penalty

Capital of the World." Holmes, who doubled the number of lawyers in the DA's office, wrote for *Texas Monthly* after his retirement that he never let the criticism of overzealous capital punishment bother him. "If you don't like our ways, don't commit murder here," he wrote.

During Shelton's time as a prosecutor, he argued for and received a theft conviction against Edgar Arnold, a Black City of Houston employee. On appeal, the court found that Shelton improperly struck seven Black people and one Mexican person from a pool of potential jurors.

But by that time, Shelton was on his way out. After his three-year stint in the DA's office, Shelton moved on to the law practice of a traffic-ticket attorney named David Sprecher, whom the *Houston Press* called "the acknowledged king of the municipal courts." Sprecher was known for combing the details of Houston's traffic laws—as well as schmoozing with cops and other lawyers—to create a booming business out of traffic tickets. It was a lucrative niche, and Sprecher was roundly regarded as a bizarre personality: one judge told the *Press* that Sprecher "would do well to slip on a feedbag of Valium."

But Shelton had grander visions than traffic court. He ran for a seat on the bench of the 313th District Court with the support of Steve Hotze, an ultraconservative power broker in Houston whose flyers listing his approved picks for judges were make-or-break for Harris County Republicans for decades. Hotze was a stout conservative Christian who strongly opposed abortion and backed a "Straight Slate" of anti-LGBT candidates in the 1980s.

Tim Fleck, a longtime Houston journalist, took a keen early interest in Hotze. He wrote in 1996 that Hotze employed some "un-Christlike methods" for maintaining control of judicial appointments in Harris County. For more than two decades, Hotze wielded a sixty-thousand-strong army of Republican voters who relied wholeheartedly on his political flyer during elections. He'd pull endorsements for judges mid-campaign in favor of other, more conservative candidates, Fleck wrote, and many candidates wouldn't know he'd made the switch until they saw smear campaigns directed at them, paid for by Hotze's political action committee.

Hotze spent the ensuing decades moving further to the right. During the summer 2020 protests over the death of George Floyd at the hands of a Minneapolis, Minnesota, cop, Hotze left a voicemail for Texas governor Greg Abbott's chief of staff—obtained by *The Texas Tribune*—in which he asked to send the governor this message: "I want to make sure that he has National Guard down here and they have the order to shoot to kill if any of these son-of-a-bitch people start rioting like they have in Dallas, start tearing down businesses—shoot to kill the son of a bitches. That's the only way you restore order. Kill 'em. Thank you."

In the aftermath of the 2020 presidential election, in which Donald Trump baselessly alleged there was a widespread voter fraud conspiracy, a former Houston police captain ran an air-conditioning repairman off the road with his truck and threatened him at gunpoint. The former cop, Mark Aguirre, was searching for evidence of widespread voter fraud in Harris County, and the repairman was described by the DA as "innocent and ordinary." Aguirre had been paid more than a quarter of a million dollars by the Liberty Center for God and Country, whose CEO is Steve Hotze, to pursue evidence of such fraud.

"Those summoned to kiss his ring encounter a tough, uncompromising zealot who is used to getting his own way," Tim Fleck wrote of Hotze in 1996, two years after Shelton took the bench with Hotze's approval. It's unclear why Shelton wanted the job. Unlike many in the small world of CPS and juvenile cases, where attorneys are on a first-name basis with judges, he was an outsider. "No one knew who Shelton was before he came in," one longtime CPS attorney, Margaret Lombardo, said. "He was a municipal court guy."

Whatever his motives, it was immediately clear that Shelton would take a novel approach. His court coordinator handled the administrative tasks for the judge, including maintaining the list of attorneys whom Shelton could choose to appoint on cases. Just after Shelton took the bench, Lombardo says his court coordinator took her out to lunch. "He said, 'Here's our plan,'" she recalled, outlining a scheme that shocked her in what she felt was a blatant flouting of ethics: Shelton was looking to give ten attorneys the lion's share of court appointments. "We want to raise a hundred thousand dollars from ten attorneys," she remembers him telling her, "and we're picking you! What do you think?"

Lombardo was aghast. At that time, judges had full discretion over the selection of attorneys for defendants who could not afford their own lawyers. In CPS and juvenile cases, nearly all of which involved families in poverty, these appointments had become a form of currency, since there were court-appointed lawyers assigned to virtually every case. In CPS cases, all children got a lawyer appointed on their behalf, all parents could get their own lawyer, and attorneys could even get appointed to look for fathers in cases where they were unknown; as a result, the judge had an overwhelming capacity to create work for attorneys who had knowledge of family law. And Shelton seemed to understand the power in that. Lombardo understood that the judge was asking her for $10,000, and if she didn't pay up, those appointments—the way she earned her living—would be harder to come by.

JoAnne Musick, who used to represent the county in CPS cases, agreed with Lombardo's assessment. "If you didn't contribute to the political campaigns, you were taken off the list," said Musick, who went on to become a prosecutor in the office of DA Kim Ogg, elected in 2016. "If you didn't work your cases out fast enough or get the solution the court wanted—if the court wanted to adopt a kid out but you objected to it— you're slowing it down, you're the obstructionist. Rather than look at it like the attorney may be doing their job and the placement might not be appropriate."

Judge Shelton disputed the accusations of pay-to-play at the time. "I don't choose who shows up in court. Any attorney who has a license can practice in the court," he said in the *Houston Press* in 1999. "If somebody shows up in court and tells me they want to do a court appointment, we consider everybody. It is not a closed show."

Shelton's personality was abrasive, and his courtroom

flamboyant. He used thousands of dollars of county funds to purchase vintage flags celebrating Texas's wins in battles with Mexico bearing such famed slogans as "Come and Take It" and "Liberty or Death."

Shelton liked to bring an atlas to the bench, multiple attorneys remember. He'd drill Hispanic mothers on where they came from and then, flipping to the page in the atlas that showed their hometown or province, say things like, "That looks like a great place. Why don't you go back there?" Such was the courtroom where the Davis children's fate would be decided.

Of course, racism in the child welfare system wasn't unique to Shelton's courtroom. "Family destruction has historically functioned as a chief instrument of group oppression in the United States," writes the legal scholar Dorothy Roberts in her book *Torn Apart: How the Child Welfare System Destroys Black Families—and How Abolition Can Build a Safer World*. In the 1860s, for example, the United States adopted a program of forced removals of Indian children from their families. "Steeped in Victorian gender ideals and cultural evolutionary racial models, authorities expressed great concern about how Indian children were raised and condemned Indian women's mothering and home-making skills," the history professor Margaret D. Jacobs wrote in *American Indian Quarterly* in 2013. "By removing Indian children and reeducating them within boarding schools, officials claimed they could solve the so-called Indian problem, defined at that time and ever since as the dependence of Indian people on the government."

The children were rounded up en masse from reservations and sent to boarding schools for the explicit purpose of "immersing the Indian in our civilization," according to Richard Henry Pratt, the founder of Pennsylvania's Carlisle Indian Industrial School. In a speech he gave in 1892, Pratt expressed his goal for the Native American: "Kill the Indian in him, and save the man." The idea at the boarding schools was that, for Indian children to thrive, white educators had to force them to abandon their native languages, speak English, and adopt Christianity. These places existed in some form or fashion until the 1970s, and are a main reason additional federal protections for Native American children exist in the child welfare system today.

Other groups of children faced systemic racism as well. Prior to the creation of orphanages in the United States, destitute children were sometimes rounded up and imprisoned with adults. In the 1800s, a boom of new charities focused on housing orphans in newly formed institutions. These orphanages, though, focused on poor white children, including the massive influx of immigrant children from Ireland and Italy. Black children were excluded from them until, in 1836, the Association for the Benefit of Colored Orphans was started in New York. As Roberts writes in *Torn Apart*, "Child-saving advocates established institutions for 'dependent children' and 'juvenile delinquents' simultaneously." Black children were often shuttled to the latter.

In the early 1900s, white feminist activists pushed for aid for widowed mothers, resulting in the creation of mothers' pensions. These pensions came with the requirement that mothers keep a "suitable home." This requirement was wielded against Black mothers seeking monetary support—in 1931, only 3 percent of the pensions went to Black mothers. As the civil rights movement arose at midcentury, widowed Black mothers finally became more likely to receive pensions, though as that happened, less and less money became available. The "suitable home" laws became more stringent—in 1960, two states went so far as to direct welfare workers to push mothers to relinquish custody if they were denied benefits. The next year, Congress provided federal foster care funding through Title IV of the Social Security Act. As a result, the removal rates of children from their homes exploded.

Meanwhile, there was rising public awareness of a disturbing phenomenon: the battered child. As radiologists began studying bone fractures in children, the media began focusing attention on child abuse and the psychological characteristics of abusive parents. In 1973, the Child Abuse Prevention and Treatment Act passed, authorizing federal funds for the prevention and treatment of child abuse. Much of that funding went into investigations, and as those investigations exposed apparent dangers in the home, the number of foster children continued to balloon—from 177,000 in 1961 to 503,000 by 1978.

At last, some began to wonder if child removal had gone too far. The Adoption Assistance and Child Welfare Act of 1980 required states to make reasonable efforts to keep children at home and to return those in foster care to their parents.

But the political tide turned again. By the time the Adoption and Safe Families Act was passed in 1997, a number of other federal policies made Black families particularly vulnerable to coming under the surveillance of the child welfare system. Welfare reform was a major driver. In 1996, Congress passed Bill Clinton's Personal Responsibility and Work Opportunity Reconciliation Act, which drastically reduced welfare benefits and made them contingent on employment or employment training. During the debate over the act, Newt Gingrich, then Speaker of the House, proposed banning any woman who had a child before she turned eighteen from welfare benefits for the rest of her life; the savings, he said, could go to building orphanages to house those women's children. The double whammy of welfare reform, which made it much harder for mothers in poverty to receive assistance, and new sentencing laws, which sent waves of people to prison for extended periods, hit Black communities—and families—hard. Those developments, along with the sped-up timeline for processing and resolving cases due to ASFA, had a lasting effect on a generation of Black children who were legally severed from their families.

By the time the Davis kids' case reached Judge Shelton's court in 2005, Black children in Texas were almost twice as likely to be reported as victims of abuse or neglect than white children. They were also removed from their families at a higher rate, spent longer in substitute care, were less likely to be reunited with their families, and waited longer to get adopted. Shelton's court, though, seemed to go beyond the legacies of institutional racism—the judge could appear deeply hostile, particularly to the Latino families who came before him. And some who pushed back on his antics quickly found themselves out of work in his courtroom.

In 1999, Shelton was presiding over a juvenile case involving fifteen-year-old Sergio Reyes, accused of tussling with security guards while attempting to shoplift. Shelton asked the boy's mother a series of humiliating questions, including, "You've been in this country twenty years and you can't speak English?" When Shelton pulled out the atlas, Reyes shouted that it was his case and urged the judge to leave his mother alone.

Reyes punched Shelton's bailiff in the chest; that part is undisputed. At that point, Shelton later testified, he flew down from the bench and physically restrained the teen, an account supported by two of Shelton's favored lawyers—his high school buddy John Phillips, now taking appointments in Shelton's court, and Phillips's law partner, Glenn Devlin. But another witness said Shelton got to the boy after he was already restrained and "gratuitously shoved him in the back." A Hispanic court translator named Carlos Conde later testified to the judge's hostile treatment of Reyes's mother; after that, Conde reported that he was banned from getting assignments in Shelton's court.

"The kid started fighting with my bailiff. Had nothing to do with Mexico," Shelton said years later. "My best friend lives in Mexico. A country I'm very fond of. So what can I say?"

"I'm not saying Pat Shelton is 100 percent racist, but there is too much smoke for there to be no fire on this,"

Joel Salazar, the president-elect of the Mexican American Bar Association at the time, told the *Houston Press* after the trial. Salazar said those who wrote off Shelton's behavior as "a good ol' boy judge who doesn't mean any harm" were engaging in "Klannish thinking."

Salazar was responding to what he saw as the real downplaying of Shelton's tactics by many in his courtroom, who relied on his appointments to make a living. Attorneys who worked in Shelton's court at that time, nearly all of whom were white, seemed to have a high tolerance for his outlandish behavior toward nonwhite children and families.

Even JoAnne Musick and others who vehemently opposed Shelton's court appointment practices tended to minimize any racial aspect of Shelton's decisions. Musick admitted that his atlas antics were more or less "an ethnicity issue," but she hedged when it came to Black families. "It's hard to say if there's a true bias, because the bulk of the cases are Black children in that court," Musick said. "Partly due to the fact that typically your lower-income-housing person doesn't hire their own lawyer."

One thing that everyone in Shelton's court agreed on was that the judge prized quick resolutions to cases above all else. "Anybody who speaks to you at any length about Shelton will tell you the man is obsessed with efficiency, with speed," Elmer Bailey, the former head of the Harris County Juvenile Probation Department, told the *Houston Press* in 1999. Shelton refused to reset cases for delays, and attorneys felt pressured to wrap up cases on previously unheard-of timelines. When Reyes's case was in front of a judge, it came out that Shelton had been charging families $150 in cash to appoint an attorney in his court—he did this to Marina Reyes, Sergio's mother, even though she qualified as indigent and therefore was entitled to representation for free. Shelton discontinued this likely illegal practice after it was brought up at Reyes's trial.

Shelton's breakneck speed came with some perks. After ASFA was implemented, the federal government began doling out cash to states that increased the number of adoptions they completed. The incentives were meant to reward states for finding homes for children whose rights to their parents had been severed. Most states earned very little from these incentives, but Texas was and continues to be an exception: By 2015, the state had pulled in 15 percent of the national incentives pool (some $84 million total), though it was home to only about 9 percent of the nation's population. At least 30 percent of this money was required to be spent on adoption services, but an investigation by the child welfare news site *The Imprint* found that a majority of Texas's incentive money was going to CPS for non-adoption-related expenses.

While the Texas adoption figures increased, so did something else: the state terminated parents' rights at a rate that far outstripped the rest of the nation. In 2015, Texas permanently severed 296 children's legal bonds with their parents for every 1,000 children in care; in California, which has 20,000 more foster children than Texas, the ratio was 118 of every 1,000. Between 2012 and 2020, there were more than 54,000 CPS cases in the state in which both parents' rights were terminated.

As parents' rights were terminated, children were sometimes sent out of state. Shelton was open about his hand in such transfers. "If the goal is permanency, it has to be a nationwide approach," Shelton said in an interview. "Some states have very little interest in adoption compared to others. Minnesota has been very helpful overall in providing folks who have an interest in adoptions."

When Sherry Davis and her children landed in Shelton's courtroom, his mind may have been elsewhere. Some attorneys in his court had felt that he had become distracted around that time because of his own family issues. In October 2006, Shelton's nineteen-year-old daughter, Elizabeth Shelton, was driving down Highway 59 in Houston while her boyfriend, Matthew McNiece, hung out of the passenger window, waving his arms. They were both drunk, and Elizabeth slammed the passenger side of her Lexus SUV into a delivery truck, crushing Matthew's head and killing him nearly instantly.

At the hospital, Elizabeth, whose blood alcohol level was .26, more than three times the legal limit, was inconsolable. According to news reports at the time, she told the nurse who was taking her blood sample, "My daddy is a fucking judge." The media covered Elizabeth's case relentlessly, and there was much to cover—including Judge Shelton's role in it.

Shelton immediately hired Mark Sandoval to represent his daughter, a lawyer who at that time had been sanctioned four times by the State Bar of Texas and had twice had his law license suspended, for a total of four years. Sandoval went to the public impound lot to inspect Elizabeth's crumpled vehicle before police investigators did. When investigators did arrive, they saw that the car's black box, which would have pegged the speed the car was going when it crashed, was missing. Sandoval had to be compelled to hand over the black box, and when he did, the data could not be successfully retrieved.

At trial, Elizabeth's defense team argued that the truck driver swerved into her lane and that he, in fact, was responsible for the crash. Shelton himself had a heated exchange with prosecutors, during which he told them the driver should have been charged for failing to stay on the scene—he got off the freeway at the next exit and immediately came back around—and that a witness to the crash should have been detained for being an "illegal" immigrant. "No one's above the law," Shelton told the incredulous prosecutor.

A jury convicted Elizabeth for intoxication manslaughter, and she served four months in jail. She was sentenced to 240 hours of community service, which was expected to take her thirty months to complete. Instead, a judge signed off on her community service hours as being complete as she finished her jail sentence. She'd told the judge her community service was "cleaning and passing out supplies to inmates at the jail." The sheriff's office told the *Houston Chronicle* that they'd never heard of someone being able to serve community service and their jail sentence simultaneously.

In 2008, the Sheltons sued the truck driver Elizabeth had hit for $20,000, to cover repairs to the Lexus she'd been driving when she crashed into him, plus more for "mental anguish, pain and suffering."

"With his daughter, he went off the rails," one attorney working CPS cases at the time said. "He really took it out on the DA's office, the prosecutors there, and made some really strange rulings."

The same year his daughter's story was plastered all over the local news, Shelton presided over the four Davis children's case. Shelton appointed Glenn Devlin to look for the fathers of Dontay and Devonte, a fruitless search that nonetheless earned Devlin his daily fee.

It was in Shelton's courtroom that Sherry relinquished her rights to her children. Because she gave them up voluntarily, the case was never brought to trial. Sherry's attorney notified the court of the relinquishment; in child welfare proceedings, the parents are rarely allowed to speak. The family's recollections of the day are fuzzy—they were confused and stressed, and still thought the children would end up with Priscilla.

But that was not to be. After the relinquishment, Shelton passed the case off to his associate judge, Robert Molder. It was to Molder that Priscilla made her plea to adopt, a plea that was denied.

And so it was decided. Devonte, Jeremiah, and Ciera would move to Minnesota, a thousand miles away from the only place they'd ever lived. To Shelton, this decision was a prudent one. He said that if Priscilla wanted to keep the children, she should never have let them see their mother. "We have been disappointed by so many relatives before, that act like kids are the property of the parents, and they'll say what they need to say just to get the kids back to the parent," Shelton said. "And it's not just the parent, it's whoever else in their life—typically a crummy boyfriend, especially when drugs are on the scene."

When the children were adopted by Jennifer and Sarah Hart in Minnesota, they were 3 of the 11,792 adoptions that went through in Texas in 2008. The state earned nearly $8.5 million in adoption incentives that year, an increase of $3.5 million over the year before. After that, Texas was functionally done with the children, aside from continuing to send monthly payments of at least $400 for each of the three children until their deaths. No one from the state ever checked up on them again.

4

Big-Time Small-Time Living

In June 2008, Devonte, Jeremiah, and Ciera, ages five, three, and two, respectively, boarded a plane for Minnesota. They were going from a nearly all-Black neighborhood in Houston, Texas, one of the country's most diverse cities, to Alexandria, Minnesota, a town of eleven thousand people, 96 percent of them white.

Their new mothers were two blond women, both raised in small-town South Dakota; they could pass for sisters. At their college, near the border separating North and South Dakota, they passed for roommates.

The Davis children joined an already bustling family. The Harts had earlier adopted three biracial siblings from Columbus County, an hour west of Houston, in 2006. There was Markis, a lanky almost-ten-year-old with wavy hair and a strong chin. And Hannah, tiny for her six years, with frizzy hair and a wide smile. The littlest, Abigail, was four at the time, with chubby cheeks and a long ponytail.

Like the Davis kids, they, too, had been taken thousands of miles away, from a more diverse community in Texas, where temperatures rarely hit freezing in the winter, and brought to Alexandria in March, which Minnesotans consider the coldest month, when there was still snow on the ground.

For kids who likely had never seen snow, that in itself was a shock. Photos from the time show the Harts' first three adopted children bundled up in coats, smiling huge smiles for the camera. Behind the lens was their new mother, Jennifer, an avid photographer, clicking the shutter.

Jennifer Hart grew up in the heartland, in Huron, South Dakota. The town had sprung up alongside the Chicago & North Western Railway in the 1880s, and to this day you might get stuck behind a train for ten minutes, watching freight cars filled with tons and tons of soybeans rumble by. There's a quaint little downtown, and the sunsets are expansive. Ten minutes' drive gets you out of town, along the James River or out into the hundreds of miles of plains and farmland that stretch in every direction.

Huron was and is a mostly white town: In 2000, after Jen went off to college, the population was still more than 95 percent white, and only 1 percent Black. It was very possible that Jennifer didn't know a Black person until she graduated from high school—her senior yearbook shows a virtually all-white class.

When Jennifer was a child, her father pulled her and her two younger brothers to the Zesto, the local ice cream shop, in a red wagon, and they'd bring their pet bunnies along. The children would lick their cones while the bunnies explored the fenced-in patio area behind the Zesto and the other patrons cooed at them. This was what her father, Doug Hart, remembers. But the idyllic moment might have happened only once, or at most sporadically, as Doug traveled nearly full-time for his job with the power company.

He was away a lot, so it was Deb Hart who raised the kids—Jennifer, the oldest, and Jonathan and Christopher, each five years apart. Deb and Doug were nineteen and twenty-one, respectively, when they married, and they fought a lot. "I said white, she said black. It was that simple," Doug says. "We were not meant to be together. I accepted that." The couple split when Jennifer was twelve, and the divorce was acrimonious.

Doug would still have Jennifer and her brothers sit down and make a Mother's Day card on his weekends with them, he insists, although Deb didn't return the favor. To her credit, Deb was the one parenting full-time. As Jen became a teenager, Doug says, "she chose not to exercise her visitation rights with me."

Jennifer never explicitly came out as a lesbian to her family. Doug says she never told him, and that it was not known to him when she was in high school. Her father says now that he would not have minded, noting that his middle son, Jonathan, is also gay. He points out, though, that nobody "like that" was on his side of the family, and that the orientation must have come from Deb, whose brother is gay, too.

That brother, Jen's uncle Randy Wilson, used to babysit the kids when they were growing up. He's currently serving a life sentence in the South Dakota State Penitentiary in Sioux Falls for murder. In 1993, Wilson was a twenty-eight-year-old who had just lost a bid for the city commission when he found Gordon Roettele, a sixty-seven-year-old former lover, at the home of another man. He admitted to assaulting the other man and hitting Roettele twice in the head with a hammer, killing him. Months before that, Roettele had complained to authorities that Wilson was harassing him and that Wilson had sent a letter to Roettele's wife, saying that her husband had infected Wilson with HIV.

Jennifer kept letters from her uncle Randy, written to her mother; in them, he makes off-color jokes about homosexuality and complains about his mistreatment at the prison.

In 1995, two years after a court in Hawaii ruled that legal challenges to bans on same-sex marriage could be brought, the South Dakota legislature took up a bill to ban recognition of same-sex marriages performed in other states. A South Dakota LGBTQ rights group called FACES—Free Americans Creating Equal Status—traveled across the state to campaign against the bill, which passed in the House but failed in the Senate. A year later, the state enacted a law defining marriage as between a man and a woman. "We put in statutory law what I believe the majority of people in the state believe has always been the definition of marriage," said State Representative Roger Hunt, the bill's sponsor.

"The government of this state has allowed the legislation of hate and the creation of a second-class citizen," FACES president Barry Wick said at the time. "This second class of citizen is defined by love."

Three years later, Matthew Shepard, a gay University of Wyoming college student, was brutally beaten and left to die by two other men in their early twenties. The story, intensely covered by national news media, drew attention to hate crimes against LGBT people. The case made quite an impression on people in neighboring South Dakota, says one of Jennifer's close acquaintances at the time. Shepard was just three years older than Jennifer, who was a freshman in college at the time.

Jennifer's brother Jonathan, the middle child, would leave Huron for the University of Minnesota in Minneapolis, a big city with a thriving queer community. But Jen chose Augustana University, a private Lutheran college in Sioux Falls. After one semester, she transferred to Northern State University, in Aberdeen, an hour and a half up 281 from Huron, near the North Dakota border. That's where she met Sarah Gengler, another transfer student, from the University of Minnesota.

Sarah had grown up in the tiny town of Big Stone City, a lakeside village of about six hundred on South Dakota's border with Minnesota. She went to school across the state line in Ortonville, which, at about two thousand residents, marked the more populous side of the lake. Big Stone City has no fast-food restaurants within town limits. The two towns are virtually all white—more than 97 percent. It's a gruff place, brutally cold in the winter.

The area is "big-time small-time living," Sarah's childhood best friend, Misty Tollakson Bongaarts, said. Sarah was shy in public, but goofy and silly with friends, Misty said. She remembers sleepovers at Sarah's house, where her dad, Alan Gengler, would drink beers in his recliner and watch TV, and the girls made up dances in Sarah's room to Poison and Depeche Mode. Sarah was decidedly not out as a lesbian in high school; in fact, she was engaged to be married to a male classmate, Robert Hausauer, until they broke it off before her move to Aberdeen.

It's not clear how Jennifer and Sarah met, or what led them to fall in love. Professional-looking photographs from that time show the two women posing awkwardly next to each other. They look like clean-cut and slightly dorky buddies, hair flaxen and curled at the ends with a wide-barreled curling iron, wearing ribbed long-sleeve shirts in autumnal tones. The shots resemble 1990s-era senior portraits, Jen with an extra-wide grin, Sarah's more demure. In these photos, their hands are the tell: it is as if they are embarrassed to touch. In the most intimate one, Jennifer has an arm around Sarah's waist and another one over Sarah's hand, but both of Jen's hands are balled up in fists. In another pose, Jen stands behind Sarah, but instead of holding her arms around her girlfriend, they are awkwardly folded in front of her, jutting out behind Sarah's back. The girls wear full Green Bay Packers gear in another pose, including puffy coats and mittens and matching Brett Favre jerseys, one in yellow and one in green. In one of these pictures, Jen and Sarah stand back to back, like childhood friends, Sarah looping her thumb in her jeans pocket.

Sarah was the kind of student who spent multiple semesters on the dean's list, maintaining a GPA of 4.0, but Jennifer took her studies less seriously. At one point in college, Jen was arrested for shoplifting; she told the law enforcement officers she didn't know why she did it.

When Sarah graduated in 2001, Jen dropped out of classes one semester shy of graduating and moved with her to Alexandria, Minnesota. At that point, Jennifer and Sarah began distancing themselves from their families. Jennifer no longer spoke to her father, and Sarah cut out both of her parents. Sarah's ex-fiancé, Robert Hausauer, said that was odd since, when he and Sarah were together, she and her mom, Brenda Gengler, were "like best friends."

Misty said she'd long assumed that Sarah became estranged from her parents when she came out as gay. "I was so angry at her mom and dad," she said, "because I really did think that they cut her out because she was a lesbian—there's our small town talking—and I am like, oh my God, that's rude! How could somebody do that to their kid?" But Misty, whose mother still talks to Brenda Gengler, then added that Brenda said Sarah's sexuality was not the cause of their estrangement. "Brenda said there was nothing," Misty explained. "She just cut ties with them because Jen told her she had to make a choice"—a choice, that is, between her family and her partner.

Jennifer took Sarah home to Huron in 2005 when her grandmother, Doug's mother, passed away. At the funeral, she sat at the other end of the service hall and left without speaking to her father, never introducing him to Sarah. That was the last time Doug saw his daughter alive.

In 2004, after Jennifer and Sarah purchased a home in Alexandria, they decided to adopt children through the foster care system. It's possible they wanted children in part because it was common to have big families where they each grew up; years later, Sarah would tell a coworker that she wished she knew she didn't have to have a big family. It's not totally clear why the Harts chose to adopt through the foster system rather than using other means of making a family—such as in vitro fertilization or private adoption. To be sure, the latter two options are both expensive. IVF treatments typically start at $10,000, and they don't always take. Private adoptions can range from $20,000 to $40,000, and often involve significant wait times.

Some people seek to adopt from foster care because they see a need; despite the intentions of AFSA, there are about 120,000 children around the country, many of them older than the Davis children, whose parents have no legal claim to them and who are waiting to be adopted from the system. Still other families choose a foster-to-adopt option, often with the express wish that the kids' parents not satisfy the requirements to reunite so that they can become the children's permanent home. This was the Harts' approach.

To expand their family this way, Jennifer and Sarah first needed to become certified as foster parents. They promptly took in a teen girl named Brie (who asked in an interview to withhold her last name). They'd later tell social service workers in another state that they had done so because Brie's mom was a family friend and asked them to help her with her troubled kid. Actually, Brie's mom didn't know the Harts; Brie had been in and out of foster care since she was in seventh grade, when her excessive absences—"I think I was in school in seventh grade maybe ten percent of the time," she says—led to social services stepping in.

Brie says her mother loved her but struggled with depression, which made it so she wasn't able to parent. "She couldn't really take care of herself. Besides showing me all the love in the world, there was really nothing else going on there," she says. "I could walk all over her because she was like, 'All right, I'm not gonna fight with you, fine, do what you want.' Which wasn't always the best thing."

Brie's first stint in foster care landed her in three different homes before she was returned to her mother. But an older boy, eighteen or nineteen, had moved into her mother's home, and the fourteen-year-old Brie was taken advantage of, she says. When she asked her mother to make the young man leave and it became clear that wasn't going to happen, she called social services herself and asked to be placed back in foster care.

That's when she went to live with Jennifer and Sarah, a couple who, she said, "seemed more like close siblings" than a romantic pair. There was no kissing, no cuddling, Brie remembers. Weeks after she moved in, however, they sat her down and made it clear to her that they were in a romantic relationship, asking her, "You know we're a domestic couple, right?" Brie answered that she had figured as much, and the Harts said they wanted to make sure that was okay with her.

It was, Brie says, but there were other things that weren't okay. Not only did Jen and Sarah not know her mother, as they had claimed later to social services, but they didn't allow her to see her mother at all. On Wednesdays, when the high school gave students an extra hour for lunch, her mother would sometimes pick her up anyway and they'd drive around a bit so that they could catch up and check in. On those days, Brie says, Jen and Sarah would know without fail that she'd left campus—their little cream house was across the street from the high school. "There were always eyes on me," Brie said.

Brie had a part-time job at Subway, and her paychecks would go straight to Jennifer. "They were like my 'savings account,'" she says. But no one would ever drop her off at work—she either needed to ride her bike or, in bad weather, take a cab. She remembers that once, after months of working, she had her eye on something she wanted to buy, and when she asked Jen and Sarah for the money, they told her there was only about $130 in the account. "I was like, 'Where's the rest of my money?'" They told her they'd subtracted her cab money from her savings. "Even still, this doesn't add up, I'm missing money," she remembers saying. "I make four hundred dollars every two weeks and you're telling me I only have some one hundred and thirty dollars left?"

The house often felt tense, Brie remembers. There were no yelling matches, no outbursts. Instead, there was silence. Jennifer would often sequester herself in her room for days around her menstrual period, Brie remembers, and Sarah, who was the quieter, more passive one, would pick up tasks around the house when Jen was in one of her moods. Used to having near total freedom, Brie felt constrained under the rules of the Hart household. She was a tomboy, but she felt pressured to dress up—once, they took Brie to the mall for a makeover, which she sat through sullenly, she says, because she was insecure and embarrassed.

Brie lived with the couple for more than a year, during which time Jen and Sarah would sit at the computer in the den—a room decked out with Green Bay Packers parapher-nalia—to scour the websites for potential children to adopt. All of them were children of color. "They would say, 'Oh! Look at this beautiful child, aw, isn't she adorable? Oh I would love to just have this child and bring her home,'" Brie, who is white, remembers.

Brie had talked over her future with the couple, who said they had a plan for her to stay with them until she turned eighteen. When Jen and Sarah began to seriously consider bringing children home to adopt, they told Brie that she was welcome to stay once the children came home to live with them.

Then came "the football incident." Jen, Sarah, and Brie joined two friends, a couple, on a trip to the Green Bay Pack-ers training camp, followed by a weekend of camping in the woods. The Harts were Green Bay superfans, and the trip to Wisconsin was excitedly planned and anticipated. Brett Favre was still on the team, Brie remembers, but he wasn't at practice that day. Aaron Rodgers was a rookie then. After practice, a throng of fans huddled at the green gate of Ray Nitschke Field, along the redbrick walls, and when the players came out to their cars, sweaty, the throng descended on the parking lot. Jennifer and Brie had brought new footballs, and joined the mad dash to come up to the players' cars and position the balls at their windows, making it easy for them to sign. They gathered a bunch of signatures this way, and then Jen and Brie, along with several other fans, approached the car of the running back Ahman Green, Jen's favorite player. Green grabbed Brie's ball and signed it, passing over Jen's and the other adults' footballs in favor of his younger fans. Then he smiled, rolled up his windows, and took off.

It was an exhilarating day for Brie, as was the entire idea of the trip, so she didn't catch on to the silent treatment at first. Jen didn't say anything to her as they headed back to their hotel, and it wasn't until the next day, when they got to the campsite, that Sarah took her to the side. "You know, she's really upset that you got that signature," Brie remembers Sarah telling her. Brie was confused; it seemed clear in the hubbub that everyone was going for the signatures, and not every player gave an autograph to each and every fan. Still, she apologized.

Jen took several photos on this trip. In one, Sarah and Brie brush their teeth in the hotel, both looking up for Jen as she takes the shot. In another, Jen's football, covered with signatures, is nestled in the legs of a black dog on a hotel bed.

In the next bed, in the background, blurry and out of focus, Brie sits in her Packers jersey, eyes downcast.

After they returned from their trip, Jen did not speak to Brie for at least a week, maybe more. When Brie walked into a room, Jen would get up and walk out. Gone were the family meals at the dinner table; Sarah made Brie her dinner when Jen was not around.

In 2005, on Christmas, Jen and Sarah flew down to Houston to meet Markis, Hannah, and Abigail, the three biracial siblings they were hoping to adopt. Jen later gushed on Facebook about the day she first met the children, and specifically two-year-old Abigail. "She was the first of my children I ever held in my arms," she said. They'd had a hard trip to Houston: the flight was delayed, and when they got to the hotel they'd booked, they discovered it had caught fire. They didn't meet the children until the next day, Abigail's second birthday. "The foster mother called Abby from the upper level. This dainty little peanut walked out, grabbed the railing, walked down the stairs, stood right at my feet, and held out her arms as a gesture to be picked up," Jen wrote. "I lifted her and she immediately nestled her head right into my chest with her tiny arms gripped around me. Genuine love oozed out of every pore of my body. I will never know what it's like to birth a child or the feeling of holding your newborn for the first time, but I imagine the feeling is much like what I experienced with Abby."

The children were scheduled to move to Minnesota in

March 2006. Two weeks before that, Brie went to her regularly scheduled therapy session with her longtime therapist. They had their normal hour, catching up on and working through things. But at the end of their session, her therapist broke the news: she wouldn't be returning to Jen and Sarah's. Instead, her caseworker, waiting outside, would take her to her new foster home. All her belongings had already been moved to her new home. The Harts didn't stick around to tell her goodbye.

Today, Brie says her mother recently told her about a meeting that had been called involving her care team, including the Harts, Brie's therapist, her caseworker, and her mother. Jen told them that they found a rope and a note under Brie's bed and they were worried that she was suicidal. Because of that, they wanted her out of the house before their new kids arrived. Indeed, in the home study conducted on the Harts while they were applying to get custody of their second set of kids, the caseworker notes that Brie was removed from their home in February 2006: "Due to suicidal idealizations and threats, Jen and Sarah didn't feel comfortable in their own house and they didn't want that negative energy to impact their children."

Brie recalled her mother's description of the meeting at which Jen told the care team about Brie's suicidal ideations: "My mom said everybody in the room was like, 'What? This is not my child, this is not the person I've been working with. But if it's not a good fit, we'll get her the heck out of there.' So they lied, yes, to get me out of the house—I have never been suicidal or homicidal."

She never spoke to the Harts again, and for a long time she thought they kicked her out because she got that football signed by a player that Jennifer liked. "I mean, that was on my mind for years: 'What happened?' *Years*," Brie says now. "It was still always in the back of my head, like, 'What did I do?'"

She saw the couple just once after that, loading their three children into the car in front of the house across from the high school Brie still attended. "When I saw the kids there," she says, "I was very hurt."

5

Across State Lines

In 1848, when Charles Loring Brace, a well-connected Yale graduate, moved from his home state of Connecticut to New York City to attend divinity school, he was surprised to see thousands of poverty-stricken children in the streets. In a book he wrote later on the early days of the Children's Aid Society, which he helped to found, he gave the following description:

> Most touching of all was the crowd of wandering little ones who immediately found their way to the office. Ragged young girls who had nowhere to lay their heads; children driven from drunkards' homes; orphans who slept where they could find a box or a stairway; boys cast out by step-mothers or step-fathers; newsboys, whose incessant answer to our question, "Where do you live?" rang in our ears, *"Don't live nowhere!"*[;] little bootblacks, young

peddlers, "canawl-boys," who seem to drift into the city
every winter, and live a vagabond life; pickpockets and
petty thieves trying to get honest work; child beggars and
flower-sellers growing up to enter courses of crime—all
this motley throng of infantile misery and childish guilt
passed through our doors.

The first flyer distributed by the Children's Aid Society
put it this way: "These boys and girls, it should be remembered, will soon form the great lower class of our city. They
will influence elections; they may shape the policy of the
city; they will, assuredly, if unreclaimed, poison society all
around them. They will help to form the great multitude of
robbers, thieves, and vagrants who are now such a burden
upon the law-respecting community."

In those days, as is true today, the category of "orphans"
included many children whose families were still living. Immigration brought thousands of families to New York, where
many struggled to earn a living wage and to support their
children. The children who ended up on the streets were often swept away to houses of refuge, poorhouses, or even adult
jails, but Brace had a different idea: he would round them up
and send them out west, where families needed extra hands
to work the fields. "We hope, too, especially to be the means
of draining the city of these children," the Children's Aid
Society flyer stated, "by communicating with farmers, man-
ufacturers, or families in the country, who may have need of
such for employment."

Brace is now known as the father of the foster care movement, and the early "orphan trains" carried 200,000 children to states out west between 1854 and 1929. Once the children arrived, families could choose to adopt or, if they'd prefer, sign contracts to provide room and board in exchange for indentured labor until the child turned twenty-one.

"Some ordered boys, others girls, some preferred light babies, others dark, and the orders were filled out properly and every new parent was delighted," one Nebraska paper reported in 1912. The Children's Aid Society planned to check on the children annually, but many of their letters were ignored, leaving the children to fend for themselves in cases of abuse or mistreatment.

Between five thousand and six thousand children on the orphan trains ended up in Minnesota, becoming part of some of the first adoptive families there. People raising other people's children had always happened informally; adoption didn't start becoming codified into American law until the 1850s. In 1917, Minnesota became the first state to require investigations of both the child and the potential family in order for an adoption to be finalized, in an early version of what is now known as a home study. At the end of World War II, the number of babies born to women who were un-married increased steeply, and because of the deep stigma attached to out-of-wedlock births, the number of adoptions saw a subsequent sharp incline. Throughout the 1950s, about 100,000 adoptions took place in the United States each year.

In the 1950s, as more adoptions crossed state lines, child welfare workers saw a need to formulate guidelines for the process. New York, in 1960, became the first state to join the Interstate Compact on the Placement of Children. All fifty states, plus Washington, D.C., and the Virgin Islands, are now part of the compact. According to the American Public Human Services Association, "The Compact ensures prospective placements are safe and suitable before approval, and it ensures that the individual or entity placing the child remains legally and financially responsible for the child following placement."

It's likely that Jennifer and Sarah Hart didn't know much about this history when they decided to pursue adoption through the foster care system and began scouring websites like the Texas Adoption Resource Exchange in search of children to bring home to Minnesota. It's unclear why they made no serious attempts to adopt children locally. They approached a Fergus Falls adoption agency called Permanent Family Resource Center, which stated that it focused on finding permanency for children in foster care, through something called concurrent planning. Concurrent planning began in Washington State in 1980, when Lutheran Social Services came up with a plan to address the increasing problem of "foster care drift," or kids moving around frequently inside the system without finding permanent homes. Child welfare agencies in those years regularly practiced "sequential planning," in which the prospect of parental reunification had to be exhausted before other plans for permanency could start. Concurrent planning, in contrast, allows social workers to work toward reunification with biological parents, which is legally mandated, while simultaneously operating a second plan for permanency, either with a relative or in an adoptive home.

The 1997 Adoption and Safe Families Act codified the pursuit of reunification and other permanency options at the same time. Now the practice is standard around the country, and some studies have suggested that it reduces the amount of time children spend in foster care. But critics point out that there's a tension between the understandable desire to help children exit foster care quickly and the recognition that it might take time for parents to reunify with their children—especially since reunification often involves completing a lengthy service plan, or attempting to maintain sobriety, under less than ideal conditions. Texas goes further than most in prizing speed—as we've seen, it's standard procedure for CPS in Harris County to immediately file for termination of parental rights when children come into foster care, even before a reunification plan is in place.

On its now-defunct website, the Permanent Family Resource Center in Fergus Falls described concurrent planning as "both philosophy and a case management method emphasizing candor, goal setting and time limits with neglectful or abusive parents," and explained that "it is based on the belief that foster care outcomes are determined as much by the agency's approach as by the parental situation."

For the Harts, fostering to adopt went smoothly. Jen and Sarah were first authorized to adopt through the agency in August 2005; by December they'd met Markis, Hannah, and Abigail. By the following March, the three children were living in the Harts' home. By that September, the children were legally adopted.

On the tenth anniversary of their adoption, Jennifer, who had taken to writing long and intimate Facebook posts for her growing followers, wrote an extensive post to commemorate the three children's first night at home. The post divulged private, and at times disturbing, details about what she claimed happened that night. The dramatic flair is indicative of the tone she was beginning to craft for her public posts, a tone that was taking hold on mommy blogs and adoption influencers' social media accounts, one of a heartfelt mother baring her soul.

"A different kind of Mother's Day. March 3, 2006," the post began, describing the apprehension she and Sarah felt waiting for the children to arrive, an apprehension that had been building for almost two years as they searched for children to adopt. "All the challenges of a lesbian couple trying to break through barriers in a rural community in Minnesota just transformed into a story of hope and triumph," she wrote.

As the social worker drove up with the children in her car, Jen wrote, "my heart pounded with pure love and the strength of a million drums as we embraced and welcomed them to their home for the first time." From there, the hopeful tone shifts to describing the first twelve hours the children were living with the couple, in which a litany of challenges befalls the family, according to Jen's recollections: Abigail urinated everywhere and fell down a flight of stairs, "resulting in a bloody gash on her chin." Hannah "pulled out chunks of hair and smeared feces on the wall and gorged herself with food until she started choking and needed the Heimlich, resulting in episodes of projectile vomiting." And Markis banged his head on a wall repeatedly, causing himself to bleed, and then told the women "he was possessed by demons as he growled, clawed, and spoke in multiple voices, while continuing to thrash, bite, and bang his head on the wall."

Jen's tale of the night rounds out by describing Abigail having an asthma attack and the family rushing to the emergency room at one o'clock in the morning. After this brutal night, Jen wrote that she had second thoughts about moving forward with the adoption. "What had we done? We had no experience with these kinds of things. We questioned everything." But ultimately, she and Sarah decided to keep the children, writing that if the adoption were to fail, the original plan was that the siblings would all be split up, with Markis sent to a residential treatment center and the other two adopted separately.

"If not us, who? At 25 years old, we didn't have any parenting experience under our belts, but we had boatloads of love, compassion, intelligence, and the natural instincts to navigate these wild and unchartered waters. There was no way on earth we were going to toss these children back into an incredibly broken and abysmal foster care system," Jen wrote. "Here we are, one decade and three more kids later. Ten years ago today, we became mothers and began the grandest adventure of our lives. Through the spectrum of despair and utter joy, I give thanks to all of us who have joined this journey of the hearts. Look what love can do. Come assist in writing the next chapter with us. Love, love, love."

There's no way to verify any of the information Jennifer shared in her post about the first night she and Sarah spent with Markis, Hannah, and Abigail; medical records are private, and there are no corroborating witnesses to this account. The claims about the children's original permanency plans before the Harts stepped in cannot be confirmed with the limited documents available in these children's CPS case files and have been contradicted in other family members' accounts. In other instances, Jen's intimate public recollections proved to be false, so at least some skepticism is in order.

But it's a fact that raising adopted children, especially children who are old enough to have memories of their birth families and of the trauma of their removal, can be extremely difficult. Far beyond "natural instincts," many of these children with complex trauma histories need therapy regimens with multiple trained caregivers and safe, supportive, stable schedules and home lives.

Sarah worked at a department store, while Jennifer stayed home with the kids. It's likely that the two new mothers were as overwhelmed as Jen described. Even so, documents from the Hart family home show that the couple was looking at another sibling group of four children, this time from Austin, as early as April 2007—less than six months after the first children's adoptions were finalized.

The sibling group from Austin didn't work out, but by the fall, Jen and Sarah had set their sights on Devonte, Jeremiah, and Ciera.

6

"If Not Us, Who?"

When Jennifer and Sarah Hart looked into adopting Black siblings, they were participating in a long-standing national drama and debate over transracial adoption. In 2005, the Harts were asked to fill out their "transracial adoption homework" as part of the process of adopting Markis, Hannah, and Abigail. "The homework was about identifying people and places in the community that minority children could identify with," the caseworker wrote in her notes. Jen and Sarah reported that there was a satellite campus of the University of Minnesota forty minutes away with a Black student union that put on campus activities. They weren't sure about churches or restaurants. They listed a grocery store, Natural Expression, which the caseworker noted was an "Ethnic Food Orient [*sic*] Store." And they had just purchased a couple of books, including *Martin's Big Words*, about Martin Luther King Jr.

By the time the Harts were set on adding the Davis children to their family, the case plan put together by the Permanent Family Resource Center noted that "Jen and Sarah are culturally competent to raise biracial and African American children." The center added that they had developed close relationships with Black community members (though it did not list the names of any), and that they had "culture sensitive toys, such as African American dolls, picture books etc."

The Hart family "has a family doctor that is aware of medical needs due to their ethnicity," the plan stated, but didn't add any details about what those ethnicity-related medical needs might be. The school the children would be attending—in a county that was 97 percent white—was reported to be "racially diverse."

Sharon Kearbey, the caseworker who placed the first three children with the Harts, wrote in a letter of recommendation, "I would have no problem placing kids of any age, race or sex in this home because I know they would be loved and cared for beyond anything I could hope to have for them."

In the decades after World War II, women were increasingly entering the workforce, living independently, and having premarital sex. Birth control was difficult to obtain, abortions weren't federally legal, and there was still a very real stigma attached to being an unwed mother. Many young women were coerced into giving up their children during this period; others voluntarily relinquished their newborns.

In *The Girls Who Were Sent Away: The Hidden History of Women Who Surrendered Children for Adoption in the Decades Before* Roe v. Wade, Ann Fessler, herself an adoptee, writes that 1.5 million babies were relinquished for nonfamily adoptions between 1945 and 1973.

During this first real adoption boom, "agencies adopted a powerful 'matching' philosophy," writes Elizabeth Bartholet, a Harvard law professor who has written extensively in favor of increasing transracial adoption. "Prospective parents were ideally to be matched with children who were physically and mentally as close a match as possible to the biological children they might have produced."

Many states enacted laws that allowed them to issue new birth certificates for adopted children, replacing the names of the birth parents with those of the adoptive parents. These policies were made with the understanding that many birth mothers wouldn't want to be known to their children later in life for privacy reasons, and many adoptive parents would not want to share with their children that they'd been adopted at all. The assumptions underpinning this policy have proved in many cases to be untrue. Many young mothers who were coerced or forced by their families to give up their children were denied any knowledge of where their children ended up. In many places, adult adoptees are still fighting to gain access to their own original birth certificates so that they can find their birth parents or at the very least know who they are.

Black unwed mothers of this period received particular scrutiny and stigma, but their children were rarely adopted. One 1952 study conducted in Kansas City, where Black people made up 12.3 percent of the population, found that less than 4 percent of children adopted in the city were Black, although Black children made up 20 percent of children in out-of-home care. Transracial adoption was still taboo, but efforts at finding people of color to adopt fell short. In New York City a coordinated effort to get more Black and Puerto Rican children adopted, called Adopt-a-Child, resulted in the identification of more than 1,000 eligible Black and Puerto Rican prospective adoptive families in 1959, but only 237 such children were adopted that year. That's because child placing agencies had the final say, and they rejected many prospective families because they were too poor, their housing was too crowded, or they had working mothers. "It was almost as if being black by definition excluded one from adoption eligibility requirements," writes Laura Briggs, a feminist critic and a historian of reproductive politics and U.S. empire, in her book *Somebody's Children: The Politics of Transnational and Transracial Adoption.*

As Native American activists in the 1960s pushed for ensuring the sovereign rights of tribes, and advocated that tribes take control of their children's education, Indian boarding schools began falling out of favor. But a 1958 program led by the Bureau of Indian Affairs, in partnership with the Child Welfare League of America, had already begun a nationwide push for the adoption of Indian children by white families. The program, called the Indian Adoption Project, was responsible for hundreds of adoptions of Native children by white families across state lines, and influenced even more adoptions through state child welfare systems. These adoptions were an early example of a coordinated push by the U.S. government to promote adoptions of kids of color by white families.

Proponents of the Indian Adoption Project—insisting that Native children, like Black children, were being overlooked in the child welfare system—appealed to a "color-blind" approach to adoptions. "During the past decade there have been many programs designed to promote the adoption of all children—the handicapped child, the child in the older age group, children of other racial groups both within the United States and from foreign lands," wrote Arnold Lyslo, the head of the Indian Adoption Project. "But the Indian child has remained the 'forgotten child,' left unloved and uncared for on the reservation, without a home or parents he can call his own."

But as attitudes shifted toward adoption of children of other races, the demand for Native babies and children increased. One study by the psychologist Joseph Westermeyer found eight cases in Minnesota in which Native parents sought welfare services for help caring for their children and instead had their children removed to the foster care system. In 1966, the Bureau of Indian Affairs put out a press release praising the Indian Adoption Project. "One little, two little, three little Indians—and 206 more—are brightening the homes and lives of 172 American families, mostly non-Indians, who have taken the Indian waifs as their own," the release began. A survey by the Association for Indian Affairs found that, by 1976, between 25 and 35 percent of Native children were being removed from their homes, and that 85 to 95 percent of those children were in non-Native homes or institutions. Those numbers prompted concern. In 1978, Congress passed the Indian Child Welfare Act, requiring child welfare systems to give preference and special protections to Native families and tribes.

Similar shifts occurred in the adoption of Black children. In *Somebody's Children*, Briggs notes that before 1975, between 5,000 and 12,000 nonwhite children were adopted by white families, and says that "some agencies and social workers, in their enthusiasm to promote what they undoubtedly saw as politically progressive measures, sent black and mixed-race children into what had to have been difficult situations, just as some of the children in the highly publicized school desegregation struggles went into unwelcoming schools and communities."

One 1974 study of 125 such families in large cities across America reported that nearly all of the families were in all-white or predominantly white neighborhoods, and interviewers found that 20 percent of the families were not fully accepting of their child's racial background. In 1972, two years prior to that study, the National Association of Black Social Workers had released a statement that strongly opposed the transracial adoption of Black children by white parents. "Trans-racial adoption of Black children," it read, "has frequently been accomplished at the expense of the parents having to sever all connections with their own families." Instead of transracial adoption, the NABSW members advocated for agencies to "alter their requirements, methods of approach, definition of suitable family and tackle the legal machinery to facilitate interstate placements" to find Black families who could take these children in.

The statement was controversial, especially for its apparent likening of transracial adoption to "cultural genocide." It is best understood within the context of the era's Black pride politics and a rising consciousness of systemic racism. "Black people are now developing an honest perception of this society; the myths of assimilation and of our inferiority stand bare under glaring light," the statement read. "We now proclaim our truth, substance, beauty and value as ourselves without apology or compromise. The affirmation of our ethnicity promotes our opposition to the trans-racial placements of Black children."

Several members of the NABSW later said that the statement, which had a large impact on perceptions of transracial adoption at the time, was mischaracterized. "The resolution was not based on racial hatred or bigotry, nor was it an attack on White parents," wrote Leora Neal, president of the NABSW's New York chapter, in 1996. "The resolution was not based on any belief that White families could not love Black children, nor did we want African-American children to languish in foster care rather than be placed in White adoptive homes. Our resolution, and the position paper that followed, was directed at the child welfare system that has systematically separated Black children from their birth families."

Indeed, in *Torn Apart*, Dorothy Roberts argues that "the systematic court-ordered displacement of free Black children to strangers' homes" began in the years after the Civil War.

At the time, Southern apprenticeship policies enshrined in the Black Codes called for forced indenture of Black children in white homes without their parents' consent. "These laws," says Roberts, "gave judges unfettered discretion to place Black children in the care and service of white people if they found the parents to be unfit, unmarried, or unemployed and if they deemed the displacement 'better for the habits and comfort of the child.'"

The 1972 NABSW statement has been credited with causing a nationwide drop in transracial adoptions. In 1983, Minnesota passed the Minority Child Heritage Protection Act, "requiring due consideration of the child's minority race or minority ethnic heritage in adoption placements." The act required that children be placed first with relatives, and then with a family of the same race or heritage, and then, finally, with a family of a different race that was "knowledgeable and appreciative" of the child's race.

But proponents of transracial adoption argued that despite the country's racist history, the disproportionate number of Black children in foster care needed help *now*, and that help was most likely to come from the surplus of white families who were looking to adopt. In a 1991 paper for the *University of Pennsylvania Law Review*, the Harvard professor Elizabeth Bartholet wrote, "It is true, as advocates of current policies say, that more could be done to find black families. More substantial subsidies could be provided and more resources could be devoted to recruitment. But it is extremely unlikely that our society will anytime soon devote more than lip service and limited resources to putting blacks in a social and economic position where they are capable of providing good homes for all the waiting black children."

Ultimately, those arguments won the day. In 1994, Congress passed the Multiethnic Placement Act, prohibiting race from being a consideration in adoptive placements. As a result, Minnesota's Minority Child Heritage Act was, in effect, nullified. In a 2006 paper titled "Cultural Stereotypes Can and Do Die: It's Time to Move On with Transracial Adoption," Bartholet argued, "It seems to me clear that MEPA serves the interests of children, by helping black children in particular to find placements in loving homes of whatever color as promptly as possible. MEPA also seems to me to serve the interests of the larger society, by combating in a small but significant way the notion that race should divide people. Race-matching is the direct descendant of white supremacy and of black separatism."

There's no doubt that many families of transracial adoptees are happy and that many children in those families are loved. But that doesn't mean the experience isn't complicated for these adoptees, says Melissa Guida-Richards, a transracial adoptee from Colombia and the author of *What White Parents Should Know About Transracial Adoption*. She says that we see "happily-ever-after" adoption narratives so often in the media largely because adoptive parents like to think of it that way. Those parents, she adds, hold the most social power in the adoption triad, which consists of adoptive parents, adopted children, and birth families.

"They're trying to encourage us to try to be happy in the family that we have and to realize how lucky we are that we're not in an orphanage, and to do that, unfortunately, there's often a lot of comparisons and things will be exaggerated about our birth families," Guida-Richards said in a February 2022 interview. "We're not supposed to think about what happened before and want to know our birth family because then it makes a lot of adoptive parents uncomfortable. And that puts a very heavy weight psychologically on adoptive children because we're being pulled in two different directions."

Guida-Richards stressed that many adoptive parents are trying their best to create a good life for their children, and some might see minimizing their child's racial difference as a way to do that. But ignoring race can leave adoptees feeling confused about their identity, with nowhere to turn when they experience microaggressions or outright racism.

In the Harts' case, the adoptive parents leaned into raising Black children, taking them to protests and aligning themselves with a multicultural message about the importance of love. "These boys live and lead with love, but I will never deny them their human right to be frustrated, sad, and angry about the perpetual violence and murder of people of color," Jen wrote in a 2016 Facebook post with a photo of her sons. "My feed is filled with people, white and POC, that want to help make a difference but are completely at a loss of what to do. Opening up and breaking the silence is a start because white silence is black death. If that statement makes you uncomfortable, I'm not sorry. Black pain matters. Black anger matters. Black lives matter."

Some aspects of Jen's approach, however, made Guida-Richards and other transracial adoptees bristle. Relaying private information about the children's mental health and about their birth families and histories, as Jen often did on Facebook, is a breach of her children's trust, Guida-Richards said. It's also an example of a concept known as white saviorism. Jen painted the children's families as awful and abusive, and the children as in need of saving. "Adoption tends to be put on a pedestal where adoptive parents can do no wrong. When a lot of transracial adoptees grow up and start to make their own lives separate from their family, there's an awakening, where we realize that we had some difficulties developing our racial identity in a white-majority family and often a white-majority area where we grew up," Guida-Richards said. "And then if we share our stories and the struggles we've had as a result, there's often a lot of backlash. 'Well, why aren't you grateful?'"

What happened to the Davis children in the court system is a direct example of how policies can be discriminatorily applied. Nationally, a typical adoption of a child from foster care can take nine to eighteen months. Both of the Harts' adoptions went quickly—they were completed less than nine months after they'd chosen the children from the Texas Adoption Resource Exchange website, and just after they'd met the six-month requirement stipulated by Texas law.

The Davis kids had not yet reached that six-month

milestone in the Hart household when one of their new siblings made a statement that suggested an incident of abuse.
Hannah Hart, who had been adopted with the first set of
siblings in 2006, went to school with a bruise on her arm.
When asked, Hannah told her teacher that Jennifer had hit
her with a belt. Both Jennifer and Sarah Hart told the police
that they had no idea how Hannah got the bruise, and that
she had recently fallen down the stairs. They said that Hannah "has been going through food issues, where she'll steal
other people's food at school or eat out of garbage cans or
off the floor." The case was closed without charges filed—
and the adoptions of the Davis children, which were still in
process, went ahead as planned.

When Elizabeth Cantu, a Texas CPS worker, came out
to the Harts' home to check on the children for their placement update the next month, she made no mention of Hannah's bruise or her teacher's call to child welfare workers. It's
likely she did not even know it happened. She also made no
mention of the pending appeal by Priscilla Celestine, who
was trying to get the children back. The placement review,
which was an important step toward adoption, was glowing.
"Devonte, Jeremiah and Ciera have healthy appetites and
love bananas!" wrote Cantu. The children had been weaned
off all medication, she noted; they were alert "and not like
zombies." She lists the fun activities the family had taken
part in recently, like fishing and going to the county fair.
"The children have appeared to adjust very quickly to the
family," she added. "Adoptive parents thought it would be
harder for these kids to adjust then [sic] their first adoption,

but it has been easier, since they have known what to expect from their first experience." Cantu's report concluded: "They are in a stable and loving environment. The children are bonding with the adoptive parents and are continuing to thrive."

Despite Priscilla's still-pending appeal of the court decision against her, the Davis children's adoption was finalized in February 2009. That same year, the whole family traveled to Connecticut, where Jen and Sarah were legally wed. (Same-sex marriage did not become legal in Minnesota until 2013, and in South Dakota until 2015, following the Supreme Court's landmark ruling in *Obergefell v. Hodges*.) In March, a month after the adoption was completed, Jennifer emailed her friends with news that the three children were officially part of their family: "We finalized their adoption last month, thank goodness. I have been a ball of anxiety just waiting for that day to come. Until a couple months ago, a maternal aunt was still trying to get them back. Long story. Happy ending, or beginning." It's unclear what Jen means when she says "a couple months ago"—the final decision denying Priscilla's appeal wouldn't be issued until July 2010.

Where the Davis family had encountered resistance in the system, the Harts were met with the benefit of the doubt. Priscilla's appeal was treated as a rejected one long before the judges made their ruling, but the Harts were fast-tracked through the process despite reports of abuse. Priscilla was denied standing to ask for an adoption because the children lived with her for only five and a half months, not the required six. But the Harts received glowing reports that

pushed their adoption along at four months, despite the call
Hannah's teacher made about her safety.

"Yes, there are children from very unfortunate circumstances or abusive homes," Guida-Richards says. "However,
many, many children are only in 'need' of foster and adoptive
placements because their parents are too poor or may be on
the receiving end of discriminatory policy, not because there
is a lack of love or problems with abuse."

7

Playing the Food Card

Six children from two sibling groups with extensive and unique trauma histories would be a lot for any parents to handle, but documents from the time show that the Harts weren't sure their family was complete. Just two months after the second set of adoptions was finalized, Sarah and Jennifer signed papers for IVF treatment. The following month, the couple was looking at twin children from Texas, one with cerebral palsy. Information on the children and their birth family was sent to them by Sharon Kearbey, the caseworker who worked on Markis, Hannah, and Abigail's case. That adoption didn't happen, though, and in July, Jennifer emailed Jodi Trosdahl, who worked at Permanent Family Resource Center, to tell her that they couldn't find a heartbeat when Sarah, who had received IVF, had gone for her checkup.

Just a couple of months after Jen sent that email, the Permanent Family Resource Center was put on a two-year conditional license after being cited for dozens of violations, including mishandling paperwork, placing a child in a home before the home met licensing requirements, and allowing staff to have direct access to children without completing background checks on the employees.

A Minnesota child welfare worker would later say that Texas frequently used PFRC to place children in Minnesota, "even when the [Minnesota] Child Welfare office has not supported the placement." According to the Interstate Compact on the Placement of Children, though, the receiving state—in this case, Minnesota—would be in charge of the home study, which determined that the Harts' home was suitable for children. The PFRC, which at one point used a photo of little Hannah kissing Sarah on her cheek in its marketing materials, would close down in 2012.

Two years after the Davis children's adoption was finalized, there were more signs of trouble in the Hart home. In November 2010, Abigail, the youngest of the first set of siblings—the one Jennifer wrote about holding in her arms on their first meeting—was inspected by her teacher, who found bruises from Abigail's shoulders to her waistline, on her stomach and back. Abigail told her teacher that her mother Jennifer had hit her with a closed fist, submerged her head in cold water, and withheld food from her. She told a police officer called to the school that the reason for the abuse was that "she had a penny in her pocket and that made her mom mad." Even though Abigail had said Jennifer hit her, Sarah was the one who was charged with assault for that incident. Sarah told the police that she lost her temper.

While that investigation was under way, Hannah's teacher called the Harts in January 2011. She told Sarah that Hannah hadn't eaten all day and that she'd said that Jennifer had shoved a banana and nuts in her mouth for being disrespectful. "She's playing the food card," Sarah responded. "Just give her water."

In April 2011, Sarah pled guilty to misdemeanor domestic violence and received a ninety-day suspended jail sentence and a year of probation. Jennifer and Sarah immediately pulled the children from school, and Jennifer began to homeschool them.

Adopting children is full of challenges, and many adoptive parents say that supportive services often end once the adoption is finalized. Many parents struggle with their children's mental health issues, including attachment trauma and often PTSD. It's easy to imagine that the Hart couple was overwhelmed, but if the stress of parenting was behind the women's increasingly alarming behavior, there were multiple off-ramps in these years that the two women didn't take. If Jen's Facebook post about her first three children's first night with them was true, then it was clear that parenting children from the foster system was much harder than they'd imagined it would be. Still, they thought "their innate mothering instinct" qualified them to care for the kids, and instead of allowing each set of children time to adjust to the new family dynamic, they quickly sought to add more and more children to their family.

The Harts pushed ahead with finalizing another chal-
lenging adoption despite the fact that they were admittedly
resorting to physical violence in an attempt to gain control
over their kids, and despite the fact that the new children in
their home had family members who wanted them. Instead
of asking for help, Jennifer became more vocal on social media, positioning herself and Sarah as saviors.

When people adopt children from the U.S. foster system,
most of them qualify for a state or federal monthly adoption
subsidy that continues to assist in the care of the child until the
child turns eighteen, or sometimes twenty-one. At the time
the Harts pulled the children from school, Texas was sending
them nearly $1,900 a month in adoption subsidies, making up
half of their household income. Despite Sarah's guilty plea for
domestic violence, there is no record that any state agency in
Minnesota or Texas considered removing the children from
their home. In fact, caseworkers involved with the Harts
seemed smitten with their ideas about parenting, writing of
Jen's insistence on raising her children with a vegetarian lifestyle, and of the Harts weaning their children off the medications they were prescribed when they came to live with them.

None of the caseworkers even asked questions of the
children's teachers, who were clearly concerned. The teachers had reported six incidents to the state's social service
agency in 2010 and 2011; those reports mainly claimed that
the children were hungry, taking food from other students
and even going through the trash looking for food. After a
while, the school stopped calling the Hart home, "because
they didn't want the children being disciplined or punished,"

a later CPS investigation notes. Caseworkers also didn't ask much of the children's doctors, even though there were instances in which the women lagged in taking the children to required medical appointments. There's no record of the Harts pursuing therapy for the children, several of whom had received diagnoses of ADHD or learning disabilities. When the children left public school, they left behind access to their teachers, as well as social workers, counselors, and nurses. After that, the only adults who would be in regular contact with the children were their mothers.

Once Sarah's probation ended in 2012, the Harts began talking about moving in earnest. In early 2013, they left town, heading west to a suburb of Portland, Oregon. They framed the move to friends as a new chapter in a progressive oasis, where they wouldn't be hounded by conservative people who didn't understand their lesbian relationship or their six Black children. "We deserve to live in a community where not everything has to be so difficult," she wrote to a friend. "Not only will it fill us with nature's endless beauty, it will satisfy our culture cravings as well."

No more abuse reports were filed in the year between the end of Sarah's probation and the family's move to Oregon. But signs continued to indicate that something wasn't quite right. In May 2012, ten-year-old Hannah got her two front teeth knocked out. Jen posted a gruesome photo to Facebook. In it, a white hand holds an entire bloody tooth, root to tip, between two fingers. "Hart House Guidelines are rather simple," Jen's post begins. "The first rule is to speak and act with kindness. And the second, no running in the house.

Rough day for daughter and mamas learning why number two is so important. Two front permanent teeth out. Poof. Blood bath. Holy horror. OUCH! Now, coping. Dealing. Healing. Today's not-so-gentle life lesson: Impermanence."

Given Jen's propensity for tall tales, and the lack of medical records surrounding the incident, it's not totally clear how Hannah lost her teeth. Jen's version of events, that Hannah tripped while running in the house, is definitely plausible, says Greg Olson, professor and chair of pediatric dentistry at the University of Texas School of Health. After reading through Jennifer's Facebook post, he said, "What she described in that little section is not uncommon for a dental trauma, just like that."

But while the story Jennifer gave about Hannah's teeth was not unusual, Olson was troubled by other aspects of the post. "Posting a picture about it on social media, that's probably a little less common. Usually the parents are horrified," Olson says. He thinks about how Hannah must have felt when that happened; it's common for kids to be in shock. "That is really traumatic, and it's painful. All of a sudden, it changes how they look."

Olson says it's not unusual for young people to wait until they've stopped growing to get permanent implants, but it isn't clear why Hannah went five years without getting a cosmetic retainer. Did she decide against it herself, or did her parents decide for her? Hannah was already tiny for her age, and that gap in her smile made it look like she'd just lost her baby teeth, naturally making way for adult teeth to come in. As it turned out, Hannah never got any new teeth. She died before then.

8

"Is It Because I'm Bad?"

Slowly, Dontay started to realize he had been left behind.

A month after his siblings left for Minnesota, Dontay still hadn't been told that they were sent out of state and that he would no longer be able to see them. He spoke to yet another new caseworker, Quindalynn Mattox, and told her he was sad because he wasn't able to see his brothers and sister. He told her he cried sometimes because he was homesick and he didn't want to be away from his family. "They kept saying the foster parents didn't want me to have no contact," he said. "I thought, 'Is it because I'm bad?'"

Life at Serenity Place, the North Houston residential treatment center where CPS placed him, was heavily regimented and, for Dontay, boring. Daily logs from his time at Serenity Place noted everything from whether or not he brushed his teeth to the number of pairs of clean underwear in his drawer. Instead of the arts-and-crafts projects and report cards a family often keeps as a way to record their child's progress, Dontay has a massive foster care file: forty-seven hundred pages of placement notes, medical and school records, and daily logs from the treatment center. There are no awards in the file, no artwork—nothing much positive at all, really. Some parts of his caseworker's daily narrative from her required monthly check-ins are clearly cut-and-paste comments. In several spots, he's called someone else's name, likely another child on the caseworker's heavy load. But the file does include, in minute detail, each infraction Dontay committed during his four years at Serenity Place. The staff wrote seventy pages of incident reports; the incidents include fairly harmless events, like when Dontay stormed out of the room after he asked to borrow a GameBoy and was told no, or when staff threatened to take away his dinner if he did not eat it quietly.

Serenity Place, like many RTCs, employed a behavior modification model: residents who exhibited good behavior got rewarded with privileges; those who exhibited bad behavior got punished with a "loss of level." Those on the lowest level often had the least privileges, and Dontay was usually on the lowest level, leaving him without privileges that other kids had. He wasn't able to play football, which he longed to do, because his behavior wasn't good enough. He felt that football would be a positive outlet for his aggression; instead, he turned again to fighting. He fought other boys constantly. "When you're in a group home with a bunch of kids, you can't let anybody pick on you," he says.

Dozens of Dontay's incident reports detail fights. One altercation with another resident landed him in front of a judge and on probation. At that point, Dontay became a "dual status youth," one involved in both the child welfare and juvenile justice systems. In 2015, upward of 50 percent of kids in the juvenile justice system nationally had also been involved with the child welfare system.

Dontay told his caseworker that he'd like to be adopted, into a two-parent family with siblings. "We discussed his behavior as a barrier," Quindalynn wrote in her notes. "I told Dontay that the agency will seek an adoptive home for him and he needs to continue working on improving his behavior."

Dontay tried, but it was a struggle. In the beginning, before he understood his separation from his siblings was final, he tried hard to behave. "I started praying, but that wasn't working for me," he said later, "so . . ." He shrugged his shoulders.

Dontay looked around at the dingy hallways, at the staff members who would twist his arms behind his back when he lost his temper, at the old gray buildings in a part of town far away from where he grew up, and he knew that he was in a place for kids who weren't wanted. "Ain't nobody wanted to adopt me," he says. "I thought if I did good, they would let me get back with my brothers, but when they didn't, I said fuck it."

Around that time, Quindalynn handed him some forms to fill out, and to her surprise, he couldn't. He couldn't read very well, he told her, and she noticed he wasn't even able to write his birth date on the form. Dontay was twelve, and in the sixth grade.

Quindalynn pressed a Serenity Place staff member on Dontay's inability to read, since he attended a charter school attached to the treatment center. She also noticed that his clothes were tattered and his shoes were ripped, even though the facility had just received his clothing voucher from CPS. "She stated she will look into this and get back to me," Quindalynn wrote of this conversation; no follow-up conversation seems to have taken place.

"It wasn't fun, it wasn't life," Dontay says about the four years he spent at the RTC. He'd make close friends, boys he thought of as brothers, but they'd move into another building or sometimes even out of the center, going home with a family. "To see people come and go—you get close to somebody, and they would get adopted."

More than a year after he had last seen his siblings, Dontay again asked Quindalynn if he could speak to them. "We did discuss him possibly not being able to talk to them again," she wrote in her notes. "I told him, that though it may be sad, he can keep the memories of them in his heart."

The problem of what to do with orphans has always existed. Technically, the word "orphan" refers to a child with no living parents, but the term has always included children whose parents are very poor or otherwise unable to care for them. Back when multiple generations of families lived together, orphans were cared for by grandparents, aunts, uncles, or older siblings. For those without extended families, the standard of living was such that many died. As the industrialization of the 1800s brought mass migration into cities, children who needed looking after spilled into the streets.

Many deemed the street children criminals. Not all had committed crimes, though, and those who did often did so to survive. These children were initially thrown into jails along with adults. It wasn't until 1825 that the nation's first juvenile reformatory was created. The New York House of Refuge was funded by a philanthropic organization called the Society for the Prevention of Pauperism, which had been organized in 1816 and called for a separate place to house youth. A statute was enacted, giving judges the ability to "commit juveniles convicted of crimes or adjudicated as vagrants" to the house of refuge. Initially envisioned as a kinder alternative to incarcerating children with adults, these houses of refuge, which proliferated around the country in the nineteenth century, were soon dealing with the same problems that had cropped up in jails and prisons: far too many children were corralled in increasingly decrepit buildings, and they experienced widespread abuse.

By the 1930s and '40s, a growing body of research indicated that living in such settings was detrimental to children. Meanwhile, the Social Security Act of 1935 helped support impoverished families who might otherwise have been forced to place children in state care. A movement was now afoot to disband orphanages and place children in more stable, family-oriented settings.

After the Great Depression, many of the sheltering institutions of the day adopted a mental health focus. The concept of residential treatment, championed by the well-known psychologist and Nazi concentration camp survivor Bruno Bettelheim, matured in the 1940s. RTCs exploded in popularity between the 1950s and 1970s, as books by Bettelheim and others extolled the virtues of congregate treatment. These psychologists theorized that both children and adults suffering from a range of conditions, from autism to schizophrenia, could be helped by placing them in a therapeutic environment full-time; such an environment could control for all aspects of their care.

Bettelheim later broke with others in his field, arguing that disturbed children needed not drugs and shock therapy, but constant acceptance and love. His practice did not match his theory, however. Bettelheim was widely regarded as one of the most influential minds in the fields of child development and psychology, but after his death in 1990 he became the subject of intense controversy. It was discovered that his credentials were fraudulent. The man who'd popularized residential treatment for emotionally disturbed youth was in fact an art history major who'd taken just three psychology classes.

Bettelheim was also posthumously accused of frequently hitting his child patients. Two weeks after his death, the *Chicago Reader* published an anonymous letter written in response to its obituary, describing life at the University of Chicago's Sonia Shankman Orthogenic School, run by Bettelheim from 1944 to 1978. The letter presented not only a specific and harrowing account of a particular institution but also a broad indictment of the harms of institutionalizing children, including physical abuse, psychological terror, twisted power dynamics, and isolation from loved ones. The letter writer claimed that Bettelheim "bullied, awed, and terrorized the children at his school, their parents, school staff members, his graduate students, and everyone else who came into contact with him" and that he "told the children over and over how lucky they were to be at his school, and that if they didn't do as they were told, they would end up in a state mental asylum where they would be given drugs and shock treatments."

Bettelheim's misdeeds were cruel, but institutional abuse has never been limited to one bad actor. In Texas, abuse at institutions for children was not just tolerated but at times encouraged. In 1967, Lester Roloff, a radio preacher with a huge following, founded the sprawling Rebekah Home for Girls in Corpus Christi. Roloff was positively gleeful about admitting to physically abusing the "wayward" girls there, whom he called "dope addicts and prostitutes." "Better a pink bottom than a black heart," he said. "We whip 'em with love and we weep with 'em and they love us for it." Girls at the Rebekah Home suffered beatings with leather straps and were isolated in locked rooms. In 1973, after two parents visiting their child at the Rebekah Home witnessed another child being beaten, a legislative hearing was called wherein girls told of terrible abuse they'd suffered and showed photos of their injuries. Just as at Bettelheim's Orthogenic School, the girls said they were cut off from the outside world, unable to contact their families or open their mail.

As a result, Texas enacted the Child Care Licensing Act in 1976, requiring facilities housing children to meet minimum standards of care. But it didn't get better for the girls in the Rebekah Home. In 1979, five girls attacked another resident with a knife, seriously injuring her, and Roloff failed to report the incident to state authorities. One of the girls involved told the *Corpus Christi Caller Times* that the girls had decided to kill one of the residents because they "hated it here" and hoped it might get them out of there. "We thought if maybe a girl would die, we'd all get to go home," she told the paper. Roloff resisted state regulation of the facility so fiercely, on the grounds of separation of church and state, that the standoff became nationally known. Roloff even spent several short stints in jail for refusing to grant licensing officials access to the property.

On Roloff's side was the first Republican governor of Texas since Reconstruction, Bill Clements, who agreed to carve out a licensing exemption for Roloff and other church-run facilities in exchange for Roloff's endorsement on his popular radio show. On the other side was a fledgling licensing agency and the cries of parents who had fetched their children from the home, many of whom crossed state lines to bring them to the Rebekah Home. After a mounting number of courts ruled in favor of the licensing agency, requiring the Rebekah Home to close, a three-day standoff took place on the ranch that *Texas Monthly* later dubbed "the Christian Alamo." The legal battle continued even after Roloff himself was killed in a plane crash in 1982.

Just as those early houses of refuge blurred the lines between youth who had committed crimes and those with nowhere else to go, institutions for children have continued to encompass a catch-all amalgam of children in various situations. The only thing that has changed, really, is the branding: Child welfare officials will tell you that no orphanages exist today; instead, children get "treatment" at RTCs, or are sent by juvenile judges to state schools for "reform" or "training." In Texas, guards at juvenile detention facilities are called "youth development coaches."

In 1995, the well-known political pollster, consultant, and pundit Frank Luntz wrote a memo to House Republicans advising them to use the term "foster homes" in place of "orphanages." This word change caused one in ten voters to change their minds in favor of Republican-led legislation, Luntz said. "In baseball terms, using foster homes rather than orphanages is a home run," the memo read.

"The orphanages of old are today's RTCs," says Richard Wexler, the executive director of the National Coalition for Child Protection Reform. "Sometimes literally—it was founded as an orphanage then dressed up in psychobabble and rebranded an RTC—sometimes only in spirit. But whatever you call them, they're worthless at best, harmful at worst."

These days, children can enter institutions in myriad ways. Each day in 2019, forty-eight thousand American children were incarcerated in the juvenile justice system; that same year, the child welfare system sent twenty-six thousand of its hardest-to-place children to institutions such as RTCs. Additionally, parents at their wits' end send an average of fifty-seven thousand kids to institutions each year; the "troubled teen" industry rakes in up to $1.2 billion annually. These numbers are huge, but they represent a marked decrease since 2010, when thirty-six thousand foster children lived in institutions and seventy-one thousand were incarcerated through the juvenile justice system. The decrease is partly due to a widespread body of research that shows institutionalizing children harms them.

Still, in Texas alone, thousands of kids like Dontay end up in RTCs. The state places more kids in institutions than any other, including California, even though California has twenty thousand more children in its foster care system than Texas does. In 2010, more than forty-eight hundred Texas children were placed in these facilities. RTCs are meant to be a last resort, according to the Office of Juvenile Justice and Delinquency Prevention, a federal agency within the U.S. Department of Justice, which says the facilities are for children who "have proved too ill or unruly to be housed in foster care."

Nationally, nearly 70 percent of kids in RTCs are thirteen or older, and many have been in the foster care system for years, bouncing from place to place and accumulating trauma and behavioral problems along the way. An RTC placement is a black mark on a child's case file, scaring away potentially interested families and labeling a child as "hard to deal with." Researchers at the University of Illinois determined that youth with at least one group home placement are 2.5 times more likely to become delinquent than youth in other foster placements, and that those who have experienced trauma are at greater risk for further physical abuse when placed in group homes versus family homes.

The poor outcomes make sense when you consider that RTC staff receive minimal training and are paid as little as $10 an hour. Many facilities have few or no trained social workers, making them unequipped to handle challenging children with developmental trauma. Turnover is high, and staff members are known to hop from one facility to the next, even after being let go for abusive behavior toward children. "Trauma-informed care, this can be advanced stuff," says Will Francis, the executive director of the Texas chapter of the National Association of Social Workers. "And just hoping that someone with a high school degree and minimal training and minimal job prospects can do this—that's a lot to ask."

In February 2009, Dontay, then twelve, was assaulted by a staff member at Serenity Place. The incident was reported to licensing, but when Quindalynn asked Dontay what happened, he wouldn't say a word, and the case was dropped. During his time at the treatment center, the fear of CPS Dontay had held on to ever since he and his siblings were removed had hardened into something else—hate. He didn't feel safe at Serenity Place; they weren't going to let him leave, anyway. He wasn't going to snitch, and he sure as shit didn't trust CPS to help him if he did.

But it was deeper than that, Dontay says now. He remembered the incident clearly. During a restraint, a big female staff member pulled Dontay's arm back so hard that she dislocated his shoulder. He had to wear a sling for weeks. But he thinks he was partly at fault, since he said he resisted restraint. His assessment of what happened is likely colored by who the woman was to him: she was one of the only staff members who had taken an interest in him. She noticed he never got presents for his birthday or Christmas because he wasn't allowed to have contact with his family, and she bought him Nikes to wear instead of the busted cheap shoes the facility wanted him to wear. To Dontay—who lay in bed at night wondering where his siblings were, who hadn't spoken to his mother since before he tried to kill himself two years prior, and who had no idea the man he thought of as his dad was still trying to see him and bring him presents—those Nikes felt a lot like love.

The pairing of traumatized youth with staff who are unqualified to treat them is a recipe for abuse—and abuse is rampant in RTCs. In 2015, a federal judge found that the physical, emotional, and sexual abuse routinely experienced by Texas children in long-term foster care, like Dontay, violates their human rights. The lawsuit exposed squalid conditions in RTCs, where kids are often prescribed multiple psychotropic medications and are routinely abused by staff and other residents.

The class-action lawsuit also shed light on the state's system for investigating abuse. The licensing standards that were instituted back when Lester Roloff was fighting his "Christian Alamo" in the 1970s have become increasingly complex. Unlike kids in family homes, kids in foster care today rely on a separate state agency, Residential Child Care Investigations, to look into reports of suspected abuse or neglect. That agency has a tendency to downgrade abuse reports without ever investigating them. During four months in 2019, the agency ruled out nearly half of the more than nine hundred abuse reports it received—*with no investigation whatsoever.*

In contrast, when an allegation of abuse is made against a child in a family home, CPS sends an investigator out to look into the complaint in every single case. Up until 2017, there were two separate definitions for "abuse and neglect" in Texas—one for most kids, and another, more lax, for children in foster care. "Fundamentally, the state is supposed to err on the side of child safety by investigating situations that are ambiguous or uncertain," says Paul Yetter, an attorney representing children in the class-action lawsuit against Texas. "And they've chosen a policy that's basically the opposite of that."

The lax investigations and licensing standards of RTCs have resulted in children's deaths. In February 2020, for example, a fourteen-year-old girl died at an RTC called Prairie Harbor, west of Houston. The girl, who had diabetes and hypertension, had complained of leg pain for weeks but went untreated until she collapsed one night in the bathroom. Staff waited thirty-seven minutes to call 911, believing they needed approval from a supervisor to do so; the girl later died of a pulmonary embolism. The facility was closed—but the owners of Prairie Harbor were granted a license by the state to open a new treatment facility in Corpus Christi.

Tara Grigg Green, an attorney who serves as the executive director of the Foster Care Advocacy Center and represents Harris County youth in complex child welfare cases, calls making a complaint against an RTC "an exercise in futility." Children who are labeled "problem kids" are often not believed. "The RTCs don't take it seriously; they don't actually believe that they're going to be punished or held accountable," Grigg Green says. "It's always spun in a way to make the child a liar and also responsible."

Children often refuse to report abuse in RTCs, for fear that staff will retaliate against them and make their lives worse. Or, like Dontay, they don't trust that anybody will care enough to help them.

Children who live in RTCs are often on a fast track straight through juvenile detention centers and on to adult prisons. A study of 175 alumni of the Texas foster care system, ages twenty-three to twenty-five, found that 68 percent of the male respondents were involved in the criminal justice system in the years after they left foster care. The average number of placement moves for participants in the study was eleven, making it likely that many of these alumni spent time in an RTC. Grigg Green says kids placed in RTCs learn "institutional behaviors," such as a distrust for authority and the need to protect themselves against threats, often with violence—the same behaviors they might pick up in jail or prison. The more time spent in an RTC, Grigg Green says, "the less likely you'll be able to function in the community."

In the fall of 2010, Dontay was released from Serenity Place into a therapeutic foster home, a specialty designation earned by foster parents who receive extra training to care for children with specialized needs. His foster mother was a Black woman named Debra Roberts.

Dontay took a liking to Miss Debra, as he called her. She would sit with him at her kitchen table and help him with his reading; by ninth grade, he was reading at a fourth-grade level.

He still fought, and he still skipped class. But Miss Debra saw a deep pain and longing in him, one he masked with aggression and rage. She remembers him crying at times because he missed his family. "I wouldn't say his behavior was extreme," she said. "You have to get behind it to see why he behaves that way every day. And for him, it was the hurt and the pain of not being with his siblings."

Miss Debra lived south of Sunnyside, and Dontay began to notice familiar landmarks of his old neighborhood as he rode in the passenger seat of her car. One day, he skipped school and walked toward Nathaniel Davis's house for what felt like a hundred miles, into the 610 loop and up to Theresa Meat Market, a butcher and grocery store directly across from Nathaniel's apartment. Knowing that his dad used to frequent the store, Dontay waited outside for a while, until finally he saw his old man limp up and push through the shop's doors.

Dontay walked in behind him and called out his nickname. "Joe Boy!"

Nathaniel turned around and said, "Now, who callin' me?"

Dontay was fourteen, his voice much deeper than when

Nathaniel saw him last, six years earlier. Nathaniel wobbled where he was standing, nearly falling for a moment, and started to cry.

Later that night, after Dontay had spent some time at his old apartment with his mom and dad, Nathaniel dropped Dontay off at the end of his foster mother's street. Dontay walked home, wearing a new jacket his dad had given him, and Debra noticed that. "Where have you been?" she asked him, and he dodged the question.

Debra had a feeling, and she checked his home address in his paperwork. "I said, 'You're not gonna get in trouble, just tell me where you went.'"

So Dontay took Miss Debra back to Nathaniel's house, in the very same apartment he and his siblings had lived in years ago, when the boys would leave the new bunk beds empty and climb into Nathaniel's bed instead. Nathaniel, again, was in tears, Miss Debra remembers. "He said, 'Miss Debra, I always just knew these kids would come back to me.' He never stopped looking for the kids, he sure didn't. He never stopped looking for those children."

Miss Debra was cautious at first—she told the agency that Dontay had found his family, and his caseworker warned him that if he ever went back there, they would remove him from Debra's home. Dontay promised he wouldn't return, but he promptly told his caseworker that he no longer wanted to be adopted. "He fantasizes of returning home," she wrote in her notes.

He started asking his caseworker, again, about his siblings—what was their address, their phone number? He told her when he turned eighteen, he was going to go look for them. He began to lobby to have visits with his parents; she told him there was no way to do this, since their rights had been terminated, but he didn't stop asking. After several months, she told him she would ask her supervisor.

No more family visits were recorded, but Debra concedes that Dontay did begin to see Nathaniel and Sherry, and as she slowly got to know Nathaniel, she came to trust him. "He's a great parent," she said. "It could've went another way, where he could've adopted the kids."

Debra also began to ask the caseworker if Dontay could have sanctioned visits with his family. She told the caseworker that Dontay talked about his father all the time, and was always emotional when he spoke of him. Nathaniel was seventy at the time, and Dontay was worried something bad would happen to him before he could be with him again.

In one visit to his caseworker, Dontay broke down crying. Miss Debra nudged the caseworker again. She said that all he needed was to talk to his siblings, to know that they were okay.

Dontay was single-minded in his wish to return home to his family. When Dontay went up for placement review before the court, his attorney told the judge that Dontay wanted to be back with his father. His foster mother, Debra, agreed. The judge decided to give custody of Dontay to Nathaniel when Dontay was sixteen, just two years shy of aging out of the system.

It was a happy outcome, but it did not undo the damage that had been done by Dontay's childhood away from his home. His ability to trust, or to believe in a future for himself that included being safe and loved, was broken. By then, Dontay was skipping school at Jack Yates High most days and wearing red, like the other boys in his gang on the block, many of whom he had met while at Serenity Place. He got a couple of trespass charges as a juvenile, and a theft charge. Then, in 2015, when Dontay was nineteen, he was arrested, charged with aggravated robbery, and convicted. He began a three-year sentence in the Gib Lewis Unit in Woodville, Texas.

"Fuck it. I don't have nothing to live for, I don't got no little brothers, I'm by myself," he says of his mindset at the time. "That's how I always felt, like I had nothing to lose."

9

Dichotomy

Sarah and Jennifer Hart spent the spring and summer of 2013 getting their family acclimated to their new home in West Linn, Oregon, outside Portland. While Sarah worked at her new job as a manager at Kohl's, Jen took the kids on several trips both near and far. In June, Jennifer and the children visited Alexandra Argyropoulos, a friend in the San Francisco Bay area. Alexandra, who went by Alex, had met Jen through Lindsay, a mutual friend who'd grown up in South Dakota, and Alex had welcomed the family warmly.

But things didn't feel right to Alex. She noticed that the children were tightly controlled by Jennifer, who punished them harshly for very minor things. Alex conferred with Lindsay, who told her about an incident that had alarmed her during a recent visit of the Hart family to her own home, in Arizona: At dinner, each child had been given only one small slice of pizza. In the morning, when she noticed the leftovers were gone, she jokingly asked her husband if he scarfed them during the night. "I can't believe them!" Jennifer said when she heard someone had eaten the pizza, immediately assuming her children had done it. Lindsay assured her that it was fine, but Jennifer punished the children by making them lie still on an air mattress for five hours. Lindsay kicked herself all day for bringing it up. (Lindsay did not want her last name included in this book.)

Alex and Lindsay talked about how the family's use of "meditation" as punishment actually entailed the use of sleep masks and long stretches of time during which the kids were made to sit still and silent. But when the friends raised their concerns, Jennifer either brought up the kids' adoption history as a reason for the techniques or simply clammed up.

Alex and Lindsay also talked about how, over the years during which they'd known the family, the children got taller but never seemed to gain any weight. They decided to make a report but were adamant about remaining anonymous. The Oregon Department of Human Services report about the 2013 call notes: "The caller said anytime anyone has confronted [Sarah and Jennifer] about their parenting approach, or said anything about the food, . . . Jen has an answer for everything, but then they will just cut people out of the world. The caller said if Jen or Sarah piece together that this caller made the report, the children will have no one, who will be able to try to advocate for them."

In July 2013, a West Linn police detective and a Clackamas County CPS worker knocked on the Harts' door at 10:30 a.m., unannounced. There were two cars in the driveway, including a gold Yukon, but nobody answered. The caseworker left a card, and several hours later, the detective drove by and noticed that the gold Yukon was no longer there.

In August, the caseworker got a voicemail message from Sarah, saying she found the business card when she was taking out the garbage. "We must have just missed each other the other day," Sarah told the caseworker. The family travels a lot, she said, and they'd gone to the coast to pick berries. The caseworker told Sarah that DHS had gotten reports that the Hart children were being deprived of meals. Sarah skirted the issue, saying the whole family was vegetarian and insisting that the children were not undernourished. Hannah was "very petite," she admitted, but they'd had her growth hormones checked and the tests had come back normal. Unfortunately, Sarah added, Jen and the children were out of town now, heading to a music festival. She herself had to work, so she'd been left home. She wasn't quite sure when they'd be back, Sarah told the caseworker, but she'd certainly let her know.

Two and a half hours southwest of Portland, fifteen minutes from the coast, sits Tidewater, a tiny town along the Alsea River. In a clearing set against a thick forest of western hemlock and towering Douglas firs, dotted with brightly colored canopies, a crowd of hundreds gathered in the August sunlight. White women with dreadlocks mingled with men in flowing genie pants and Teva sandals. Barefoot folks, skin covered with a sheen of dust, clasped each other's faces and stared intently into each other's eyes. Couples did acrobatic yoga moves in an area where rugs covered the ground. The music was an eclectic blend of what's been called world music.

In subsequent years, organizers of the annual Beloved Festival would begin reckoning with the whiteness of its audience, dropping the term "world music" and renaming its "Far Mosque" campground, which the festival's director acknowledged was "profoundly disrespectful to Islam."

Such concerns were scarcely evident in that beautiful forest on that day in 2013 as a bearded man with a blond ponytail and a colorful headband, chest bare except for several necklaces with beads, leather, and wood, sat on the single stage, under drapes of red-and-orange-striped fabric, strumming a Weissenborn slide guitar. His blue eyes stared off into the distance as he sang about his sacred grandmother. In the crowd were Jennifer Hart and her children, who'd driven from their Portland home in part to see the man onstage, the Australian folk singer Xavier Rudd.

As the tempo picked up, the crowd's energy was building—drums started pounding, and people began to dance. As the song lyrics turned to a chant, Rudd beckoned to someone in the crowd. A tiny ten-year-old, Devonte Hart, rose to the stage. He was wearing a tight zebra-print jumpsuit with a fluffy black tail attached, and his head was shaved into a short mohawk, with the word BELOVED etched down the center. Devonte immediately went to Xavier for a hug, stepping on the distortion pedals at the musician's feet. The crowd cheered, shouted, and cooed as the boy clutched the blond man across his slide guitar and began to weep. Xavier, with his arm around the boy, continued his low chant a cappella, his slide guitar out of reach between them.

A concertgoer's video recording of the interaction goes on for several minutes—it seems that the boy and man embrace for longer than the crowd expects them to. Rudd himself starts to cry, holding and stroking the boy's head. When Devonte finally releases the hug, the two lock eyes, while Rudd still sings. Little Devonte's shoulder blades jut out through the back opening of his costume. A woman in the crowd sighs deeply and laughs. Finally, Rudd taps Devonte on the shoulder, and as the singer again begins to strum the slide guitar, the boy turns to the crowd, his eyes wet, and now you can see: he's wearing a paper sign, with FREE HUGS scrawled in the colors of the rainbow.

While the kids were out of town at the Beloved Festival, Clackamas County DHS officials followed up on the tip the caller had given them. They reached out to the child welfare office in Douglas County, Minnesota, where the children formerly lived. The Douglas County caseworker had a lot to say, starting back with Brie, the Harts' foster daughter, saying that the placement didn't last long and that "one of the breaking point issues was the girl used wire hangers." The caseworker mentioned the incident with Abigail that resulted in Sarah's conviction for domestic violence, and told Clackamas County DHS about Hannah's bruise and about her teacher repeatedly calling in that Hannah was hungry, asking classmates for food, and telling her teacher she wasn't getting fed. "Whenever the parents were confronted about withholding food, or the children's complaints about not getting enough food, the couple always makes reference to the children being adopted, and being 'high risk' kids, who have food issues," the caseworker reported.

The problem, the Minnesota caseworker told the caseworker in Oregon, was that "these women look normal," and they were able to speak clearly and confidently about the myriad issues the kids presented with when they were adopted, including that they had "mental health issues related to food." After Jennifer and Sarah give this explanation, the caseworker said, "people tend to assign the problems to the children."

The Minnesota caseworker ended the call with a warning: "Without any regular or consistent academic or medical oversight, and unknown child welfare reviews through State of Texas for either foster/adopt subsidies, these children risk falling through the cracks."

By the time the Clackamas County caseworker set foot inside the Hart family home for the first time on August 26, nearly six weeks had passed since the county had received the reports from Hart family friends Alex and Lindsay that the children were being undernourished and abused. When the caseworker arrived, all six children were sitting at the kitchen table, coloring. At first Jennifer and Sarah bristled at the caseworker's request to meet with each child individually, but ultimately they agreed, although the couple still insisted on being interviewed together themselves. Devonte, who volunteered to go first, was the most talkative and outgoing. The other children were more reserved, "showing little emotion or animation," the caseworker noted. Markis expressed gratitude to his adoptive moms for changing his life. None of the children reported being abused.

As for Jennifer, she was "adamant that many of the family's issues stemmed from others not understanding her family's alternative lifestyle." She dominated the conversation with the caseworker and appeared more outspoken than her wife. She spoke passionately about teaching love and compassion to her children. She talked of doing yoga with the children and disciplining them through "meditating for five minutes."

In the DHS report, Jen's statements are followed by notes on what her friends who'd reported the suspected abuse had said. They'd alleged that Jen "views the children as animals before they came to her, and she as their savior." She was reported to have said Hannah came to her "morbidly obese," and the women said Jen wouldn't allow anyone to wish happy birthday to Markis on his birthday in July. One of the women said Jen "likes to parade the children around and stage them for photographs, but does not provide affection or attention beyond this."

The Harts were required to bring their children in for physicals, a sequence of appointments that usually took three months. The doctor noted that all the children, save Jeremiah, were so far below the normal curve on growth charts that their heights and weights were not listed. Because there weren't complete medical records for the kids, the doctor had no baseline height and weight measurements for comparison. Despite the children's small sizes, "the doctor had no concerns whatsoever with any of the children." The caseworker told Alex and Lindsay that the alarming details they had reported and the substantial CPS history in Minnesota still weren't enough to substantiate maltreatment. The case would be closed.

Around this time, the family began to raise their public profile. Although the kids rarely saw another adult in their daily lives, Jen posted frequent photos of the children gardening, raising chickens, and reading books in the woods. This was the homeschool experience Jen advertised. Both Oregon and Washington require homeschooling families to report themselves, but neither state has a record of the Harts doing so. The photos, though, were idyllic. Jen snapped group photos at national parks the family traversed. Often the children would meet a host of their parents' friends during the music festivals and other trips Jen and the kids took. Many of these friends were into peace and love and "free hugs"; they often remarked in wonder at the beautiful multiracial family with the extremely well-behaved kids. Many of these people speak only of Devonte; he seemed to be the children's ambassador, the public speaker. He was also, according to Jen's friends, the golden child, the only one she really talked to, and the one who got special privileges.

In contrast, Markis and Hannah seemed to get it the

worst. In the abuse report, Lindsay mentioned seeing her drag Markis inside the house, yelling that he had screamed at and hit her, though the friend had seen neither of these things take place. And Hannah, without her two front teeth, weighing about fifty pounds and standing at three feet seven inches at age twelve, was more than a foot shorter and nearly forty pounds lighter than a typical girl her age. Many of the Harts' friends simply thought she was much younger than she really was.

Some of Jennifer's Facebook posts about her children, stressing their benevolence in the face of discrimination, strain believability. In one from 2014, Jen described an exchange that she said took place at the grocery checkout line, in which an elderly man and the checkout clerk both express astonishment that her son isn't into sports. "I have never met a kid that looks like you that doesn't play sports," the checkout clerk says in Jen's account. "They all do!" the old man replies. When the boy says he is not going to play sports, he's going to inspire people instead, they ask him how. "I'm going to be myself. No matter how much people try to make me something I am not."

That encounter made it into a blog on a New Zealand–based site, and was republished on *Huffington Post*'s contributor platform later that year. "A young boy who was born into a life of drugs, extreme poverty, danger and destined for a bleak future is defying stereotypes in the most remarkable way. And his latest encounter at a grocery store is bound to open your eyes, widen your mind and capture your heart," the blog post reads. The story tells of Devonte, claiming that he "entered the world 12 years ago with drugs pumping through his tiny newborn body" and that "by the time he was four years old he had smoked, consumed alcohol, handled guns, been shot at and suffered severe abuse and neglect." The writer goes on: "It was a life with little hope and a future that seemed over before it began. That is until Jen Hart and her wife Sarah entered Devonte's life and adopted him and his two siblings seven years ago."

Jen, who is quoted throughout the piece, seems to be the source of the information about Devonte's childhood. Some of the claims are definitely false—Devonte did not test positive for drugs at his birth, and his family was never investigated for physically abusing him or his siblings. The other claims, about his lifestyle as a toddler, cannot be corroborated by the children's foster care file or by any memories from the children's birth family. "That stuff they just made up," Devonte's mother, Sherry, said.

Whether or not the stories were true, they certainly caught the attention of people who were eager to showcase Jen's preferred narrative of the children and their lives. Two weeks after the New Zealand blog item ran, Devonte would hit the big time. Just before Thanksgiving, Devonte starred in "The Hug Shared Around the World," the viral photo of the twelve-year-old clutching a Portland police officer while tears streamed down his face. "It was one of the most emotionally charged experiences I've had as a mother," Jen wrote on Facebook about the viral hug. "My son has a heart of gold, compassion beyond anything I've ever experienced, yet struggles with living fearlessly when it comes to the police and people that don't understand the complexity of racism that is prevalent in our society."

In her Facebook post, she goes on to set the scene: Devonte, bravely stepping up to the cop he feared and telling him that police brutality made him cry. The officer sighing and saying, "I know, I'm sorry." And the two sharing a spontaneous hug, one that happened to be captured by professional news photographers at a public protest event. The cop, Bret Barnum, remembers it somewhat differently. On CNN, he told the anchor that he noticed the boy crying, called him over, and the two chatted about life and art before hugging. "It solidifies what most all of us do this work for, this job for, is just to create goodwill and to help mankind, help our fellow citizens in our community, and that's what police work is all about," Sergeant Barnum told the anchor.

The photo was widely shared as a vision for racial harmony, with some who saw it not even realizing that it was taken at a Black Lives Matter solidarity protest. Others saw the photo differently, even at the time. In *Caste: The Origins of Our Discontents*, the Pulitzer Prize–winning journalist Isabel Wilkerson wrote that she was immediately unsettled by Devonte's face: "People saw what they wanted to see . . . People saw a picture of black grace when what the world was actually looking at was an abused hostage."

The image looks spur-of-the-moment; the emotion is obviously genuine. But several photos taken from other angles by other photographers that day show a scrum of photographers catching the shot. In one, you can directly see Devonte's face as he approaches Barnum. He is clearly in distress. In another, taken shortly after the hug, you can see Devonte looking directly at Barnum, who is clasping the boy's hand, as Jen, with her arm around her son, pulls him away.

The next spring, the Harts moved to Woodland, Washington, half an hour north of Portland. Jen had posted several times on Facebook about the attention the family had received after Devonte's photo went viral. She said that the boy was swarmed by fans who wanted an autograph when they went into the grocery store on an errand. But she also told friends and strangers that they got threatening emails and that reporters camped out at their house.

Jen's family is adamant that the Harts suffered harassment. One family member recalls a trip to a zoo during which a stranger made offensive comments about Jen and Sarah's sexuality and the race of their children. Police investigators have mentioned the harassment, too, though there's no evidence in the forensic investigation of the Harts' computers that was shared with the media of any abusive emails. In June 2017, Jen came back from a six-month Facebook hiatus listing an incredible number of hardships her family had recently endured, from the deaths of pets and friends, to cancer and surgery, to robbery and vandalism. No evidence of these events, besides the death of a cat, appeared in her emails or in the search of her home. But it was clear to family friends that the Harts were increasingly isolated. The family often met friends at crowded public events, but they usually canceled one-on-one plans, sometimes several times in a row.

Sometime in the spring of 2015, a real estate agent had told the Harts' Woodland neighbors, Dana and Bruce DeKalb, that a family with a lot of children was moving in, but months passed before the couple actually saw any of them. The DeKalbs shared a driveway with their new neighbors, in a heavily wooded and somewhat rural area outside the town's borders. They wouldn't meet them until one night, after they'd gone to sleep, when they heard banging at their front door.

A small girl, maybe five or six, they thought, was standing in their doorway, wrapped in a blanket, her hair tangled with twigs and leaves. She'd jumped from the second-story window, she said, and she needed them to hide her. "They whip us with a belt," Hannah told a stunned Bruce. Hannah ran past him, into their house and up the stairs to the couple's bedroom, waking Dana. "They're racists, and they abuse us!" Dana remembers Hannah telling her.

It wasn't long before the Hart family was out searching for Hannah, calling her name and flailing flashlights toward the darkened yard. Jennifer and Sarah barged into the DeKalbs' home, the couple told reporters, searching until they found Hannah upstairs in a bedroom, hiding between the bed and the dresser. Jennifer asked to speak to Hannah alone; Dana let her. When they came downstairs, Hannah's eyes were dull, and she stared ahead as she muttered an apology at Jen's behest.

Early the next morning, the family rang the DeKalbs'

doorbell. All the kids were there, and Dana says Jen launched into an hourlong speech about how the kids were "drug babies," and how Hannah's mom was mentally ill. She said Hannah was twelve, surprising Dana, who thought she looked much younger. But Hannah was actually sixteen at this time—a good decade older than the DeKalbs initially assumed her to be. Jen refused to let Dana speak to Hannah alone; instead, Hannah handed her a note. *Dear Dana Bruce* [sic]*, I stopped this morning because I felt awful about disturbing your peace and worring* [sic] *you in the middle of the night.* Hannah wrote that she was upset about the death of their cats and that she was frustrated with her brother. *I'm sorry for telling lies to get attention.*

The DeKalbs did not report the incident to CPS because they said that Jennifer's explanations were convincing. "She sold it well," Dana told the reporter Lauren Smiley, whose September 2018 article in *Glamour* detailed the events. A couple of months after Hannah had come to them for help, Dana told her father, who lived out of town, what had happened. Alarmed, the eighty-year-old man called 911 himself. He told the dispatcher that his son-in-law didn't want to get involved by calling the authorities, but that he believed the children were being "highly abused." Months had passed by the time he made the call, and after a cursory call to the DeKalbs, in which Dana had no other incidents to report, the Clark County Sheriff's Department dropped the matter without visiting the Hart family.

The DeKalbs still felt queasy about their encounters with Hannah and Jen, though, and Dana especially kept a watchful eye on the house next door. They occasionally saw Devonte pulling the trash out from the big slate-gray home, or lifting heavy bags of soil in the garden before abruptly returning to the house. The DeKalbs never saw any of the other children.

During this time, the Harts were almost completely isolated. Sarah still reported to work full-time, and her coworkers noticed she seemed stressed and particularly sensitive to the needs of her wife. Jen spent hours and hours playing a video game called *Oz: A Broken Kingdom*, her chats with other players making up nearly all of her interactions with the outside world.

On a Wednesday in March 2018, Bruce DeKalb was in his yard when Devonte stopped by and asked for tortillas. Bruce didn't think much of it, and went and grabbed some from the house. Days later, though, Devonte was back, asking for more. He started coming frequently and at odd times, asking for peanut butter and protein bars and cured meats and fruit. He never came inside the house, despite the DeKalbs urging him to. Dana, concerned, began to grill him about what was going on at home. Devonte admitted that the children weren't getting enough to eat; he told her that what Hannah had said when she came to their house was the truth. Dana says Devonte asked her not to call the cops, because he didn't want the siblings to be split up.

After roughly ten visits from Devonte in the span of three weeks, Dana DeKalb finally called Child Protective Services, and on March 23, a Washington child welfare worker knocked on the Harts' door. The family's Yukon

SUV was there, but as had happened in West Linn, no one answered. The worker left a card.

After getting no response, a Clark County deputy again came by on March 26. The card in the door had been removed; the Yukon was no longer there. A low cinder-block wall next to the driveway had been backed into and toppled. The next day, after the deputy came back, again to an empty house, the police department got word from the California Highway Patrol. The Hart family was dead.

In a YouTube video Jen posted on November 21, 2012, the day before Thanksgiving, Devonte, Jeremiah, Ciera, and Abigail sing along to a song playing quietly in the background. The children are dressed in multiple layers in what appears to be a bedroom in their home. Jeremiah sports a mohawk and a faux-fur vest; Devonte wears a bandanna around his neck and holds a small bongo drum. Ciera wears a shiny turquoise vest and a backward cap. The three dance and sing while Abigail sits below them, awkwardly holding, but not playing, a guitar. The song is from one of Jen's favorite bands, Nahko and Medicine for the People. The children sing, their voices flat, about "giving thanks for all creation," followed by a line that repeats over and over: "We are so provided for, we are so provided for."

The Nahko and Medicine for the People album on which that song appeared, *On the Verge*, was likely a favorite in Jennifer's gold Yukon, where the kids may have learned the words. Jen is even pictured in Facebook photos with Nahko from one of the festivals she traveled to in order to see his band play. Nahko had met the children, and they shared a bond: Nahko himself, who is Puerto Rican, Filipino, and Native American, was adopted by a white family in Oregon.

Several tracks down on the album, there's another song, called "Mr. Washington." It's an up-tempo tune with an acoustic guitar intro. It begins by introducing Mr. Washington, who, along with the singer, lives "with no real direction." But the next lyrics, delivered quickly in a nasal tone, paint a troubling—and familiar—image:

Dreaming of the day we drive our cars into the ocean
And all the people looking on will wonder what to say

PART II

10

"Kiss Your Mama"

Shonda Jones was working at her desk in her office in downtown Houston when something about the horrifying tragedy on the local news playing in the background caught her eye. She'd seen the broad strokes of the story a week before: Two white adoptive moms. Six Black kids. Deadly plunge off a cliff. "I didn't know them as Hart, so that's why it didn't initially ring a bell," she says. A lawyer with experience in family law, she had a special interest in stories like these, involving children who had been adopted. But working in the child welfare courts had come to depress her; her clients were often parents of children involved in the child welfare system who she felt were talked down to and berated. She also felt patronized by judges. "You're trying to go in there and do something that would help these kids, and it's almost like you're looked down upon," she says.

She'd stopped taking these kinds of cases, mostly, focusing on custody and personal injury cases, but she never quite got the bad taste out of her mouth she'd acquired in the Harris County CPS courts. Shonda had recently watched a documentary called *Missing Threads*, about the history of Indigenous children being forcibly separated from their families and cultures—at one point in the 1970s, a study by the Association of Indian Affairs reported, one in four Native children were removed from their homes and nearly all of them were placed with white families. As a Black woman, Shonda saw a lot of parallels to her clients in these CPS cases, who were also largely Black. She felt that Black culture, too, was something that Black children who were removed from their families often lost when they were adopted by white families.

The photo that flashed across the news as she watched had gone viral. She had seen it in passing years before, when it first made the rounds, but this time she lingered on it: the Black boy dressed in a brown leather jacket and a blue patterned fedora, tears streaming down his face, the white cop, whose motorcycle helmet shield is pulled up, revealing a kind of beneficent—or, she wondered, slightly patronizing?—expression.

The photo didn't sit right with her. "He was crying there," she said. "This little boy was just in so much pain and so much need for love."

Something else about the story of the crash struck her.

The reporter mentioned Houston and Minnesota and the name Devonte; these things combined rang a bell. *Could the children who died really be those same kids?* she thought, growing distressed.

Shonda Jones is a busy lawyer, fielding dozens of cases at a time, and so it was only much later that night that she had the time to dig back into her files. In a bustling law practice, paperwork can start to take over, and typically, after three years, she'd call her former client and ask them to pick up their files, and if they declined, she'd shred them. But even though this one was from a decade ago, the case had bothered her so much that she'd had an instinct to hold on to the files—she knew she had them somewhere.

It was one of the cases that had turned her off taking child welfare cases in her practice. She'd felt railroaded in the courtroom when she fought on behalf of her client, Priscilla Celestine. She got the distinct impression that she and her client were on one side, and that the county attorney, as well as the attorney appointed to represent the children and the judge, were on the other. "I felt that they double-teamed me, and that there was a harshness [in the way] that they dealt with me personally and with Miss Celestine," she says. She says the judge's bias in this case felt palpable. "If you come from privilege," she explained, "and you respect money and power, and the people in your court don't have any of that—it's unconscious and sometimes conscious racism and classism.

"They think they are doing a service," she says of the judges. "People become desensitized, it becomes like an assembly line, but you get this feeling that they think, 'You shouldn't have had any of these kids.'"

When Shonda found the file she was looking for that night, her heart sank. It was late—probably near midnight—when she picked up the phone and called her former client, Priscilla Celestine. She wouldn't usually call someone in the middle of the night like that, but she felt she had to tell her right away. Priscilla was groggy at first, but when she realized who was on the other end of the line and heard the tone in her former lawyer's voice, she quickly realized why she must be calling. She didn't even let Shonda get the words out; she told her to call her back in the morning. She got the sense something terrible had happened to the children she'd lost. The mistake she'd made that day, letting Sherry watch the children, had weighed on her ever since, and she couldn't bear to know the details of what had befallen them.

Two days later, I drove down Allen Parkway, a speedway that runs adjacent to the Buffalo Bayou, Houston's central drainage artery, heading toward the apartment where I thought I might find Priscilla. I had received a breaking news assignment to go out and try to speak with the birth families of the children, after Shonda had reached out to media about the case. A reporter at *The Oregonian* had found an appeal decision that had named Priscilla Celestine as the children's aunt, the first clue about who the children were before they became Harts; *The Oregonian* sent me, a local reporter, to follow up. I knew the judges had denied Priscilla's attempt to adopt

Devonte, Jeremiah, and Ciera, and dismissed her appeal of their removal—but little more about the children's lives.

Driving along Buffalo Bayou, I was struck by the dissonance between what I was expecting and where I was headed. Houston's main bayou runs straight through the center of town before it turns into the Ship Channel, the city's bustling port, and then finally empties out into the Gulf of Mexico. The bayou system is a necessary part of Houston, a city that has flooded regularly since its inception, and now, due to climate change, gets inundated nearly annually. These waterways have long been neglected, and many of their natural edges were covered over with concrete, in an effort to tame the erosion that causes the winding creeks to move over time. Instead, the paving increased the velocity of the water flowing through the creeks, making flooding more likely along their banks.

Buffalo Bayou was spared this cement shellacking, but for a long stretch of the city's history, it, too, used to be run-down and litter-filled, like the smaller streams that feed into it. In the early 2000s, after so much drawn-out fanfare that Houstonians doubted it would ever happen, the city began a multibillion-dollar beautification effort, adding and then expanding an intricate trail system and, in 2015, establishing a jewel of a park, one designed to withstand regular flooding.

The bayou itself is now dotted with high-rise condo towers, whispered to house the mistresses of the River Oaks oil barons down the way, and if you blink you might miss the pastel-hued public housing complex among the runners and dog walkers along the bayou trails.

This complex is in the quickly shrinking Fourth Ward. Due to its proximity to downtown and the bayou, the historic Black neighborhood has been gentrified almost out of existence. Just several small blocks of the original redbrick roads, a few dozen shotgun homes, and a rebuilt public housing complex are what remains of the old Fourth Ward. Gregory-Lincoln, where neighborhood kids like Dontay used to go to school, is now a library dedicated to the Black history of the area. But much of the neighborhood has been rebranded Midtown, where the white, postcollege set live in big-box apartment complexes or mismatched townhomes and scuttle after work between bars and restaurants.

Allen Parkway Village, where Priscilla lives, was once San Felipe Courts, a looming public housing structure built in 1944. It was constructed for white veterans and their families, and it was built directly on top of the historic Freedmen's Town. Later, it became home to about two thousand mostly Black and Vietnamese residents. When the area began to gentrify in the 1970s, the Section 8 residents, who lived in federally subsidized apartments in the complex, fought hard to hold on to their homes amid a push by developers who saw the once blighted bayou as a prime opportunity to attract wealthy residents from tony River Oaks, just west down Allen Parkway. After a lengthy battle, the city compromised, in a move that disappointed tenants—tearing down most of Allen Parkway Village and putting up a set of pastel-painted apartments with half the number of residences.

Allen Parkway Village, now known as Historic Oaks of Allen Parkway, is where Priscilla has lived for decades, and it's where the Davis children lived with her for those five and a half months in 2006. Across from Priscilla's apartment, in the park abutting the bayou, is a large granite monument to the Houston Police Department, a walkable pyramid sculpture erected in 1991 to honor fallen cops. A much smaller monument exists near the management office at Historic Oaks of Allen Parkway, this one memorializing the remains of 355 Black people who were among the first settlers to the area. The original public housing complex had been built atop a graveyard, and the memorialized remains were excavated during the teardown and subsequent rebuild of the complex.

I knocked on Priscilla's door and, when she didn't answer, that of her neighbor, a young Black woman who answered in a towel and shower cap and said that Priscilla was usually at her weekly physical therapy appointment at a nearby community center around this time. I settled in to wait on the curb. I read through the 2010 appeal decision document the editor of *The Oregonian* had emailed me, in which a panel of three judges denied Priscilla Celestine's attempt to reunite with her niece and nephews. Unlike most child welfare court records, appeal decisions are public, and this one revealed the broad contours of the family's story. It laid out the facts of the parents' termination of rights, calling Sherry "a longtime crack-cocaine abuser," with "an extensive history with the agency dating back to 1985." Reading the decision, I was surprised by the judges' tone. "Apparently undeterred, the mother proceeded to have four more children," they wrote. In denying Priscilla's appeal, the judges wrote that she "had ample opportunities to present her side of the story and argue why the children should be returned to her care" when the case originally went to trial. "We see no reason why Celestine should be allowed to have yet another bite at the proverbial apple," they concluded.

I had been sitting on the curb outside Priscilla's apartment about twenty minutes when an older Black woman pulled into a spot across the street. She was in her sixties, with a round face and glasses, and she was clearly suffering from health problems. It took her a while to get out of the car; she pulled a walker from the car, unfolded it, and placed a bag of sandwiches on the walker's seat. As I made my way toward her, I noticed she was breathing quite heavily. When I identified myself as a reporter, she fell back into her car's front seat.

"I don't want to talk about it—I can't," she said. Her body seemed to deflate.

"I'm really sorry about what happened," I said, trying to catch her eyes. "I am just trying to get a sense of the children's lives, and of what happened."

"I had to block this out of my mind, what happened," she responded, clearly upset. "I'm blocking it out right now—I don't want to hear any details."

She didn't move to get up, though, and so I stayed there with her for a moment. I promised her that I wouldn't give her any details of the children's deaths. After a minute of chatting with me near her car, she asked if I'd like to come into her home.

"This sickness and death, it weighs on me. I didn't sleep,"

she said as she entered her apartment, which was cluttered, and made her way to a seat at the dining room table. The day before, she had called Sherry, to whom she hadn't spoken since the children were taken away, and told their mother that her kids were dead.

Priscilla was still a churchgoing woman, and she took solace in the idea that God works in mysterious ways. "I realized back then that I probably wasn't going to see them again," she added, "but they were alive. And now . . . it's too hard. It's just devastating."

When she took the children in, Priscilla knew that Sherry wasn't doing well, but she says the first caseworker assigned to the kids' case didn't mind their mother coming around. And although she didn't know Sherry well, and didn't condone her drug use, Priscilla didn't mind her coming around either. She was their mother, after all, and caring for the children was never Sherry's issue—the kids were always well dressed and well fed, Priscilla said. Sherry's issue was drugs, plain and simple, and her ability, at times, to care for herself.

"They got it all backwards," Priscilla said about CPS. "They should have done something with the mother, put her in rehab—but you have people here, loved ones, to take them in, and you take them away. They got it all messed up."

Priscilla suggested that I try to find Sherry's husband, Nathaniel. The air in the room was stuffy, and Priscilla's whole body seemed to be bracing for an impact of some kind. I wondered if it was the awful details of the children's deaths, the ones she refused to learn, that she was bracing against.

"Snatching people's children for nothing—for their rules," she said, shaking her head, as I got up to leave. "I be looking for a little more mercy from them."

Nestled between two infamous Houston neighborhoods, the Third Ward and Sunnyside, the strip of Scott Street where Nathaniel Davis lived wasn't quite in the bounds of either. In some circles, this neighborhood was called either OST—short for Old Spanish Trail, a major boulevard that ran through it—or South Union. But in the neighborhood, I had heard some people call this area Southlawn, for the notorious 242-unit apartment complex butting up against Cullen Middle School, which was the subject of a gang injunction filed by the Harris County Attorney in 2015. The injunction attempted to ban ninety-two Black men from a two-mile area surrounding the complex, which was known as a hotbed of gang activity. The idea of gang injunctions was widely promoted in Los Angeles in the 1990s, when anti-gang task forces proliferated in police departments across the country. But the tide had turned against them, as groups like the American Civil Liberties Union pointed out that they violated the civil rights of those targeted, who weren't able to visit their families who lived in the targeted zones without the threat of jail time. In 2016, amid a public outcry, the Southlawn injunction was dropped.

Scott Street, which runs from downtown through the Third Ward, along the University of Houston campus, changes in feel as you cross Brays Bayou. The street becomes more alive, with people walking—a relative rarity in sprawling Houston—toward fast-food joints and check-cashing spots and Black beauty stores.

Nathaniel Davis's gated complex is across from Navy Seafood, a tiny fish-fry place with its name hand-painted in yellow letters on a bright green background. YOU BUY, WE FRY, it says above the glass door, reinforced with burglar bars.

I found Nathaniel's door and knocked. He answered, and invited me in. He was tiny, his back hunched over, glassy eyes set within a face worn down with age. Clean cut, Nathaniel kept his gray hair clipped close to his head and his shirt tucked into belted jeans; he wore sneakers.

Nathaniel spoke in a slow drawl, his Black Texas vernacular morphing at times into a kind of unique shorthand. People sometimes have a hard time making out what he's saying, and as I sat with him, I concentrated hard on his words, asking him things several times and trying to parse from his various replies what he meant to say.

Nathaniel made it clear to me that he wasn't the biological father of Dontay, Devonte, Jeremiah, and Ciera but was the only father they had ever known. "My name is on their birth certificates," he told me. (He is listed as the father on Devonte's, at least.) As he spoke about the children, tears pooled in the inner corners of his eyes, darkening the creases alongside his nose. He told me that after he lost the children for good, he had several heart attacks.

Nathaniel took out some photos of the children that he'd kept in the house. Dontay, maybe five years old, standing at an easel with an apron over his white shirt and khaki shorts, a paintbrush in his hand. A young Devonte and Jeremiah, looking up for the camera while playing with trucks. Dontay, older, maybe eight or nine, holding his baby sister, Ciera. A much younger Nathaniel, with more hair on his head and before it was gray, crouching down and holding on to Dontay, posing for the camera. Nathaniel, with Ciera on his lap, her tiny hands clutching a doll in a golden princess dress.

Nathaniel saw the children on and off while they lived at Priscilla's, but as she appealed the initial court decision against her, he'd been sidelined in the process, he said. He recalled how, years later, Dontay reconnected with him. When Dontay was sixteen, Nathaniel obtained legal custody of him. They talked all the time about searching for Devonte, Jeremiah, and Ciera. "Some kids, when they grown, come back and say, 'Why didn't you fight for us?'" he said. "And I swear I did. We all did."

Nathaniel told me that he and his wife, Sherry, had been married since 2010 but didn't live together. It was hard to work out the nature of their relationship. He was nearly eighty, and she was forty-eight. In the time they'd been married, she'd had several children with other men. He spoke kindly of her, though, called her a "sweet mother," seemed loyal to her even from his own separate home. He wasn't sure she'd want to talk to me, but he gave me her number.

I called, and Sherry agreed to meet me the next day. It turned out she lived just down Scott Street from her husband, in those same infamous apartments that had been subject to the proposed gang injunction.

The Southlawn Palms complex was composed of two

rows of identical, squat beige buildings, nearly twenty on each side of the street, with small strips of dying grass between each of them. Many of the 240-something residents of the complex could be found on the grass outside their dingy units. Babies in diapers toddled after puppies in the courtyard; young men hung around on top of their cars in the parking lot; people nodded at one another, shouted across the way, smoked cigarettes and stubbed them out. The communal feeling was palpable and intense, as if something might pop off, and if it did, everyone wanted to be around to see what it was.

As I waited, Sherry pulled into a spot in front of her home in a gold sedan. She was still in the blue scrubs she wore to her job as a home health aide. Though small dried stains served as evidence of her work caring for elderly folks, Sherry looked put-together, with a mop of slick black curls on top of her head, the sides and back cropped close. Her eyebrows had been shaved off and drawn on in severe black lines, and she wore dark lipstick and large gold hoops in her ears.

She fumbled for her keys as she made her way to her apartment door. Behind her was her best friend, Patricia Glenn, a rail-thin older Black woman with long curly braids down to her waist and jeans with rhinestones on the pockets. Sherry's ex-boyfriend Clarence, a quiet man with very dark skin, also trundled along behind.

Clarence Celestine, Jeremiah and Ciera's biological father, loomed large, his big hands giving away feelings that his stoic face did not: clasping each other, unclasping, brushing along his gray goatee. He was wearing a black pageboy cap, a long-sleeved tan shirt that pulled tight over his belly, and brown pants with a faux Burberry print peeking out of the pockets.

We were still settling into Sherry's apartment when two young kids banged on the door. "Candy, miss?" they asked, and she went and grabbed the mini Starburst packets she kept on top of her fridge.

The whole thing took just a minute; she smiled at them, and it was clear this was part of a routine. But when she shut the door, her neutral face melted into tears, and her best friend grabbed her by the arms. They held each other in the dimly lit kitchen, wailing and crying. "My babies are gone," she sobbed, with Patricia crying just as loud.

Clarence shifted in his seat, rubbing his hands together, eyes looking everywhere but at what was happening in the kitchen. The apartment was old but clean, with the kitchen leading into the living room, where Clarence sat on the couch. The air was thick with grief. They still remembered the children as small, the way they were when they last had known them. Devonte, whom they called Baby D, was the smart one, Sherry says, thoughtful, always watching. Dontay and Jeremiah were more physical, wanting to tackle each other and play. And Ciera, who was just about two the last time they saw her, loved to carry around a little pink purse and dress up.

Sherry's grief was still shrouded in shock. She had found out about the crash just two days before, when Priscilla called her—more than two weeks after it happened. "If she hadn't found out," Sherry said, referring to Shonda Jones, "I don't even think they would have told me. They haven't told me yet; they haven't called or nothing."

Clarence lived with his sister Priscilla now. None of them had heard news of the children since they were removed from Priscilla's apartment just before Christmas in 2006. "She told them, 'Kiss your mama,'" Sherry remembers of the social worker who ushered the children into her car that December day. "That was the last time I saw them."

Sherry hadn't seen the viral photo of her son hugging the cop until Patricia had told her about it after news of the crash broke. When she looked, she saw the face of her son in distress. "That should've been a happy moment," Sherry recalled thinking. "I believe he wanted to speak to the officer, but was probably too scared."

Clarence shook his head, his long fingers tangled together in his lap. "When I get home at night, it's hard to go to sleep. When they're talking about it, I want to get away from them," he said. "I don't understand why they took the kids from my sister."

"And gave them to monsters," Sherry added.

Patricia, who had moved next to me on the couch, told me to look up a judge, right then, on my phone. "Judge Pat Shelton—white man," she added.

She had a good reason to remember the first judge in her best friend's decade-old case: He was the same judge who had taken temporary custody of her own children, and was behind the split of many families in the neighborhood. "He was all on TV at the time," she remembered. "His daughter killed somebody."

Patricia was sure that race had something to do with all the missed opportunities to save the children from abuse. "If the shoe was on the other foot," she said, "we'd be up under it."

Sherry was exhausted, shocked, and in tears, but she had one request of the officials who hadn't even called her with the news. "Tell them I would like to bring them home," she said, "so they could bury them close to me."

At the end of July in East Texas, long past the bearable part of summer, the car struggled in the heat. The bluebonnets and Indian paintbrush at the sides of the road had long since given way to wild sunflowers and Indian blanket, and the air-conditioning vents blew lukewarm streams of air as the white-hot sun beat down, without a cloud in the sky to buffer it. It had been months since any of Dontay's family members had made it up to see him at the prison where he was still serving his sentence for robbery. The prison was in Woodville, an hour and a half northeast of Houston. No one but Sherry had reliable access to a car, and after visiting him once, Sherry refused to go again.

I told Nathaniel I would take them. He left his apartment dressed in a spiffy blue-and-white plaid shirt neatly tucked into his belted jeans, with sneakers and a ball cap. It took him a while to get into the car—his knee was acting up, badly swollen and uncomfortable to bend into the small space between the car seat and the dashboard. At Sherry's house, Dontay's girlfriend, Peaches, and his two-year-old

son, Ye, were waiting to get picked up. After loading the toddler into the car seat, the family was on their way, passing
through downtown and out the other side, and then, to the
outer suburbs beyond sprawling Houston. Finally the big-box
stores along the freeways began to recede and the loblolly
pines took their place. No one complained about the heat.
Peaches put her headphones in, one in her ear and one in her
son's, and they both focused on the screen of her phone.

As I drove up Highway 59, Nathaniel reminisced about
his life. Born in the ranchlands outside Brenham, Texas, in
1941, Nathaniel was a country boy, and he always felt most
himself out in the open pastures like the ones passing by outside the car window. He had grown up in a segregated Texas.
His family moved to the Fourth Ward in 1943. His mother
had thirteen children; Nathaniel was the fourth. His father
was an all right man, he said, but his mother, Rose, was really
special. On Fridays when his daddy got paid, he'd stay out
late drinking and carrying on, and if he came back home and
tried to get aggressive with his mama, the children would
jump on him in a pack. Once, his oldest sister hit their father
in the head with a glass bottle. He stopped messing around
with their mama after that, he says, still laughing when he
thinks of it.

Nathaniel lived in the Fourth Ward when many Black
folks in Houston did, and when, because of segregation,
their options were limited. He was there before Interstate 45
was built through it; he remembered the mayor coming to
the neighborhood to announce the highway's construction.
He grew up hearing from his mother about the Camp Lo-

gan Mutiny, in which an all-Black battalion of army soldiers in Houston rose up in response to humiliating, racist treatment by white police officers in 1917. The uprising and subsequent response resulted in sixteen deaths, including that of five cops. Afterward, nineteen Black soldiers were hung and fifty-three were given life sentences in prison. The specter of racial violence always existed in the background of daily life then, Nathaniel said, but much of the inner city was hospitable to Black people in those days. You knew the neighborhoods you couldn't go to, and you stayed with your own kind of people.

Nathaniel had spent nearly all his life in Houston, and more than a decade in the apartment where the kids once slept under his roof. But he imagined a quiet country life, or at least a single-family home, where he could live out the rest of his years. First, of course, he'd need to get Dontay out of prison and back home with him. Then he'd have to break the news to him that he knew would crush his spirit. And finally, before that quiet life could commence, he'd need to help his son find stability, maybe a job so he could get a place of his own where he and Peaches could raise Ye together.

Peaches and her son weren't listening to Nathaniel's plans and dreams; the toddler and his mama were dozing on and off in the backseat. You wouldn't have thought it could get any hotter, but arriving at the prison, which was on a barren patch of land with no trees to shade the beating sun, everyone began to sweat. The ground looked bleached, the grass yellow, and the sun in the cloudless sky glared off the cream-painted cinder-block walls of the buildings making up the

Gib Lewis Unit, which were shrouded in fences, barbed wire strung across the chain-link fence in horizontal rows from top to bottom.

Nathaniel almost wasn't allowed in, since he was using a temporary paper license while his plastic one was being replaced. Just this time, the corrections officer told him; don't try this again. While we waited for visiting hours to begin, I saw a long line of men, nearly all Black and brown, in white jumpsuits and shackles, headed single-file to the visitors building. From the parking lot, you couldn't pick out which man was Dontay, and the solemn line gave a depressing idea of what life was like on that parched land and in those cinder-block buildings.

Nathaniel spent two hours with Dontay, and Peaches stayed even longer, feeding Ye and his daddy snacks from the machine. The family had been worried, driving up, that someone might have told Dontay the news about his siblings—it was a national story, after all, and didn't they have TVs in the prison? But he hadn't known, after all, and his family didn't tell him. Better to wait, they thought. Better to get him home first. They felt it was the right thing to do. Still, it hurt them to hear his most urgent plan, which he mentioned several times during those brief visiting hours: when he got out of prison in October, Dontay told his family, he was going to find Devonte, Jeremiah, and Ciera.

11

"The Last Little Hope I Had"

I first met Dontay through letters. I wrote him shortly after returning from the prison and asked if he would be interested in sharing his story. I was careful not to mention his siblings; I told him I had written about others like him who had lived in foster care, and I included some of those stories for him to read. A couple of weeks later, I got a letter back. It was handwritten in ballpoint pen in a childlike script, with little circles instead of dots on the *i*'s. The sheet had been folded in thirds with the top third torn off; on the back of the lined sheet was a blank grievance form from the prison.

Hi am Dee thank you for doing a story on me and my life I know wen you here my story I know you gone cry its stuff I never told nobody. I never had nobody care about what I been throgh so thank you agin. O I put u on my visit list so you can com see me now. So how old are you if you don't mind me asking and can you shoot me some pics of you and food you know stuff you be doing in the world. I might be asking for to much im sorry, all am saying is I be whating to see the world, so wen we talk can we go out to eat or some. I pay for it im not tripping. Oh I would like to reed your articles, do you have kids are you married I realy have non to talk bout so I guss in gone tell you wright back oh can you com see me this weekend like last time with my dad thank you wright back soon wen you get this letter oh can you tell my dad to put some moe money on my book I need it

When Dontay got out of prison that fall, he returned to Nathaniel's apartment on Scott Street. Nathaniel wanted Sherry to be there to break the news to Dontay about his siblings, but she wouldn't show. So Nathaniel finally told Dontay himself.

Dontay listened, but he didn't cry. He just went cold. His tears had dried up long ago, he says; these days, he can't really cry at all.

When we first met, I picked him up, along with Peaches and Ye, and brought them to an IHOP near Nathaniel's house, off Loop 610. I noticed that the wide smiles of his siblings aren't duplicated on his face; Dontay is a serious person, often scowling, and when he gives you a well-earned smile, it comes in the form of a slight upturn in the corners of his mouth. He is compact, maybe five foot nine, with dark brown skin and black-ink tattoos that you can't really make out. He's muscular and often shirtless; he loves to play basketball with his friends down the way. When he dresses up for a night out, you'll often see flares of red, his gang color, which is prominently displayed by many young men in the neighborhood. He wears extremely tight jeans, many of them frayed, and loud two-piece matching sets with bright patterns.

Dontay was clearly overwhelmed at the restaurant; he'd never been there, he said, and it seemed like he hadn't been out to eat much at all. Ye got a kid's pancake plate with loads of whipped cream and sprinkles, and Dontay was visibly uncomfortable with his toddler son making a mess.

I made my pitch to him there at IHOP: Your story is important, I told him. I know these things are hard to talk about, and that you barely know me, but I want to help set the record straight. There were four siblings, not just three. Your life experiences matter, and people should know your story.

He got up and walked out of the restaurant. "He just be stressed out," Peaches said, and I told her I got it. After ten or fifteen minutes, when he hadn't come back in, we got the server to box up his food and cleaned the whipped cream off Ye's hands and face.

Dontay was sitting out on the curb, smoking.

"Are you okay?" I asked him.

He nodded.

"We don't have to do it now," I said. "We can do it when you're ready."

It would take almost a year of hanging out with Dontay for him to open up to me. He doesn't trust easily, or at
all, really—there were times we'd get close to a real conversation, and he'd back out. We'd set a time for me to come
talk, and when I showed up at Nathaniel's, he'd be gone with
no sign of when he'd return. One day, he called me on the
phone. "What good does this do me, now, to tell my story?
My brothers are dead," he told me matter-of-factly.

Dontay was guarded, often quiet. With no word about
where he was going, he'd get up and walk outside to smoke—
and to calm his feelings. We went slow. When I'd come down
to Nathaniel's, we'd mostly just hang out. I'd pick up Dontay
and Ye; once we went to Emancipation Park in the Third
Ward and I watched Ye play on the playground while Dontay
shot hoops with some strangers. Other times he'd blow me
off and I'd sit in the living room with Nathaniel, who vented
about his worries regarding his son.

For one, Nathaniel said, Dontay hadn't been on any psychiatric medications since he left the prison. Nathaniel was
worried that he wouldn't take them, even though he needed
them. His moods were unstable; he'd spend days in bed.
Once, Nathaniel heard rustling in the middle of the night.
When he went into the kitchen, Dontay was there in the
corner, eating a raw pork chop. "Why don't you fry that up?"
Nathaniel asked, horrified. Dontay told him that he was used
to eating it this way; as a child in the treatment center, if he
was hungry at night, he had to sneak to eat anything.

"What did they do to him in there?" Nathaniel said,
shaking his head. Nathaniel would return to this moment

many times; it's lodged into him, like the memories of losing Dontay's siblings.

Meanwhile, Dontay's relationship with Peaches was getting increasingly volatile. She would scream and holler in Nathaniel's tiny apartment, and Dontay would punch holes in the walls. Dontay would go out and not say where he was going; Peaches would try to chase him down and fight the girls he'd been spending time with.

In January, Peaches got pregnant again. Three months later, Dontay was charged with assault on a family member for throwing her to the ground in an argument. In June, Peaches lost the baby, who was stillborn months early. They named her Ron'Niyah.

Two weeks after Peaches lost her daughter, I took her and Ye to Cleburne's, an old Houston cafeteria that served fried chicken and roast beef and pies. She wasn't talking to Dontay at the moment, but she was in agreement with Nathaniel: "Dontay need help," she said seriously. In the middle of lunch, Ye got up and ran out—Peaches chased him down and found him in the parking lot. He was four now, and still tiny; his braids dangled on the sides of his head and, like his uncle Devonte, he had a big wide grin and a tendency to ham it up, doing dance moves and smiling mischievously.

Peaches was overwhelmed. She and Ye had been staying with her mom for a bit, and at Nathaniel's for a bit, and even, for a time, at her sister's. Peaches had a mood disorder, she said, but wasn't taking medication for it, either. Ye fell asleep in the car seat on the way home, and Peaches woke him up when I dropped them off, on a side street near Southlawn

Apartments. He blinked for several minutes, totally unsure of where he was.

When Nathaniel told Dontay that his siblings were dead, whatever chance at a new life he might have been hoping for upon his release was flattened under the immense weight of grief. "I was like, *Fuck life. Fuck God,*" he said. We were sitting in my car, parked out in front of his dad's apartment. After nearly a year, he was finally ready to talk, and we talked so long that my car battery died and the neighbors had to help jump-start it. "That was the last little hope I had in my life, you know? I had that hope that I was gonna see my little brothers again, one day we gon' kick it. I used to cry sometimes thinking what we could be doing growing up."

Now, when he felt anything at all, he felt rage. Dontay was extremely depressed, lashing out at the people closest to him and putting himself in dangerous situations. Nathaniel called me frequently, worrying about where Dontay was and who he was with. He said Dontay had told him that he wanted to go be with his brothers and sister. Shocked, I asked Nathaniel what that meant. "He wanna die," he replied.

"All my life, I felt something was off and people weren't telling me the truth," Dontay said in the car. At his first foster home with his brothers, he bristled at his foster mother acting overly familiar with them. "She used to tell them, 'I'm your mama,' and I'd tell my brothers, 'That's not your mama. You know our mama,'" he said. "They didn't like that, that I knew the truth, and I saw everything that was going on."

It's true that he did want to get adopted, he said, but he gave up hope of that when he was still at Serenity Place. Now he sees his survival in foster care, and his ability to make it back home to his family, as a point of pride. "If you don't pay attention, you gon' lose yourself, for real. You gon' start adapting to new families, names get changed, eating certain foods . . . I never lost myself," he said. "My name Dontay Davis. I'm not changing my name, it's the name my mama gave me."

When the former Harris County CPS judge Michael Schneider heard about Dontay's story, it bothered him. Dontay was just twenty-three, but he was a former felon who had no job history, no high school diploma, and no prospects or opportunities. Schneider put some emails out among community members who might be able to help. One was Karlton Harris, a youth violence prevention coordinator at the Houston Health Department who worked with young men ages seventeen to twenty-four who were at risk of reentering the justice system. I drove Dontay up to the Kashmere Gardens neighborhood that fall to meet Karlton and discuss his goals.

Karlton had been involved in selling drugs when he was younger, and had been incarcerated for six years. The thought of his son at home helped him find a way into a different life. Now, as he raises his own six sons, he works with young men who remind him a lot of himself at that age.

Dontay wasn't really sure what he wanted to do with his life. Karlton suggested GED programs, and talked about the various pathways and programs he could hook Dontay up with. Finally, he suggested we meet with someone at SER Jobs, a reentry program close to Dontay's neighborhood.

The tour of SER Jobs went awry. As the reentry coach Markia Monroe showed him around the recently built facilities, which included a shop out back for people interested in training to do construction jobs, Dontay played music loudly on his headphones, slung around his neck instead of against his ears. At times he barely seemed to be paying attention. He stopped at a bulletin board that asked a question about goals and dreams, leaving Markia waiting for several minutes as he scrawled something on the board in pen.

Afterward, he filled out an employment questionnaire aimed at finding him a job that would suit him. But none of the options—a retail clerk, a construction worker—appealed to him. He told Markia he wanted to get his GED anyway, though. To enroll him in the GED program, she had to ask him extensive questions about his criminal history, questions that took more than an hour to complete.

Dontay seemed to lose steam after the detailed inventory of his criminal past. He got up and went outside for a smoke break. "Is he really serious about this?" Markia asked me as we waited for him. When he returned, he sat back in his chair and asked Markia if she worked for CPS. Markia laughed, thinking the question was playful, and admitted that she used to be a caseworker. When Dontay heard that, he completely shut down. He didn't trust her anymore.

On our way out, we passed the message board. "This year is my year," Dontay had written on it, and underneath that, "For the taking." And then he signed it *Dontay Davis*, in the handwriting of a child.

Dontay went to several GED classes at SER Jobs, but he eventually stopped going. The fancy new building was only twelve minutes away from Nathaniel's house by car, but Dontay didn't have a car. It was nearly an hour each way by bus, if the buses were running on time. Plus, he didn't really get what they were asking him in the classes; he felt stupid, and he gave up.

Dontay, with no car or cell phone or computer, would have a hard time climbing out of poverty anyway, but with a criminal record and no work history, that hole felt insurmountably deep. And what was on the other side? A minimum-wage job at McDonald's? Dontay knew the boys on the street still, and there was a place for him running the same schemes that got him caught up before.

Karlton Harris says it's pretty common for young men like Dontay to drop out of programs designed to help them. All the barriers to good jobs, and all the other barriers that exist out in the world outside the program, are part of the reason, he says, but there is another: they have been deeply hurt at a young age, and they don't know how to deal with it.

"For most of those young men, the experience of the trauma that they have faced . . . Just imagine it going untreated, from a foster care system where the child may have a feeling of abandonment, right?" Karlton says. "So they already feel like they're not worth anything because, 'I've gone through the system. I've been tossed around. Nobody loves me, nobody wants me. I'm just another number, I'm not really a name.' You know?" He then adds, "I tell people you have to put yourself in their shoes in order to understand the way that they feel. Because their perception is their reality. You know, what's normal to them may be abnormal to us, but it's their coping mechanism, and this is the way that they normalize things that are really abnormal."

When Dontay entered an adult prison at nineteen, he became someone with lived experience in the child welfare, juvenile justice, and adult criminal systems. Many of the systems that could now help him as an adult remind him too much of CPS, the entity he blames for the destruction of his family and the death of his siblings. He doesn't even want to go to the doctor. Nathaniel has tried and failed since Dontay was released from prison to restart his son's disability benefits, which were halted when he was incarcerated. To get back on disability, Dontay needs to submit to a physical and psychological assessment—which he refuses to do.

"Lord, I can't make him do things," Nathaniel told me in one of our many conversations about his son. "He told me, 'I'm a grown man now, you can't tell me nothing,' and I said, 'Yeah, you right. But you're twenty-three years old and have a mind of a child.'"

More than a year after Dontay first sat in Karlton's office, I called Karlton with an update on Dontay. He wasn't able to complete the GED classes, I told him. He was blowing in the wind. It's a familiar story to Karlton, but still one that stings. "It's heartbreaking because, I mean, we've lost youth to the streets that are literally getting killed. We've lost them to, you know, catching new cases and now they're in the adult system," he says.

"You can see so much potential in the youth, but you also understand that it's a decision that they got to want to make, and a change that they got to want to make in their life," he continues. "I tell people I can talk to you till I'm blue in the face and want you to change, but change will not occur until you want it to occur. And when you ready, come back and let me know."

12

"Why Didn't They Call Me?"

In September 2018, the Clark County Sheriff's Department in Washington State began releasing hundreds of pages of court documents to the press detailing their investigation, including photos of the Harts' fridge and bedrooms, credit card receipts, copies of the paperwork found in their home, and even emails and other documentation found on their laptops.

Some of what they found was unusual. There didn't seem to be enough beds for the children in the home, for instance. A single twin bed occupied a spare room otherwise full of storage, and another room contained two small gray loveseats that likely unfolded into beds. There was also a mat against a wall in that room, with no sheets or blankets anywhere in sight.

What police found in the home at times contradicted statements Jen had made about the family's lifestyle. Instead of the all-vegetarian diet she'd espoused and Sarah had mentioned to the CPS caseworker, the fridge and freezer were full of chicken, beef, hot dogs, and lunchmeat. Multiple bottles of wine sat on the counter; although Sarah was said to have a glass here or there, Jennifer claimed she never drank. And the family that claimed to have "traded in the television for the best big screen available. Planet Earth" in 2013 had a big-screen set in the furnished basement.

From financial documents found at the home and correspondence with the Texas Comptrollers' Office, it could be deduced that when all six children were minors, the family was receiving about $2,400 a month in payments from the state of Texas. Additionally, Devonte and Jeremiah received a combined amount of over $900 each month in disability benefits on behalf of their father figure, Nathaniel Davis. Nathaniel had received disability payments from the Social Security Administration for decades, which meant that his children were eligible for family benefits. These payments never stopped coming to the boys after they were adopted, despite the fact that Nathaniel himself had not been able to see or contact the children in a decade. There was nothing illegal about this, a disability attorney confirmed; children who go on to be adopted are still entitled to the benefits until they turn eighteen. Still, it felt deeply unethical to Nathaniel, who did not understand why his disability benefits could go toward supporting the adoptive mothers while his children were being denied food and abused. It stung him even more as he struggled to restart Dontay's benefits.

The forensic digital analysis of the computer and tablet

found in the Hart home produced more revelations. Eleven different agencies, including police departments all around California, were working together on this case, but none of them could get even basic, clear identifying information from the state of Texas about the children's birth names or families. Because of a tip from Shonda Jones, the attorney, and a public appeal decision in Priscilla Celestine's case, the Davis family learned of their family members' deaths two weeks after the crash. But nearly six months after the crash, the California agencies and officers did not know the names of the birth family of Markis, Hannah, and Abigail, and neither did the media. After remains were found in a shoe on the beach in May, they were tested against DNA from Markis and Abigail's bodies, in an effort to identify Hannah. But since the three were half siblings, the tests were inconclusive.

Looking through the records in October 2018, I could see some big clues that the police had apparently overlooked. Tucked into the nearly one thousand pages of paperwork the Clark County sheriff released was the petition to adopt the siblings Markis, Hannah, and Abigail. On it were their birth names: Markis Edbert Thomas, Hannah Louise Holiday-Scheurich, and Abigail Marie Scheurich. The petition also listed the Texas counties in which they were born— Markis and Hannah were born in Nueces County, where Corpus Christi is, and Abigail, the youngest, was born in Columbus County, an hour west of Houston. I started with the name Scheurich, because two of the children shared it, and with Nueces County, where the first two were born. I went to Facebook and looked up people named Scheurich who lived in Corpus Christi. I found several, mostly white men. I began to send messages to each of them, introducing myself as a journalist along with this note: "I am looking for people with your last name who might be related to one or more siblings who are from your area. Do you happen to know a Markis, Abigail, or Hannah?"

I sent one of these messages to a woman named Trish Scheurich, on October 4, 2018, at 9:30 a.m. while sitting at my local coffee shop. This was a wild-goose chase, I figured, but it couldn't hurt to ask. Ten minutes later, Trish wrote back: "Yes I do they are my husband's grandkids," she wrote. "My husband's name is John Scheurich we have been together for 25 years, I know these children very well."

A lump landed in my throat. It seemed likely by the way she responded that Trish did not know what had happened to her husband's grandkids. I asked if I could speak with her by phone. When I called and told her what happened, she was shocked. She sketched out the basic details of the children's early lives: Their mother, Tammy Scheurich, was her husband John's daughter. Tammy was white; each of her children's fathers was Black. Tammy was a disturbed woman, Trish said, and the situation with the kids was messy.

We spoke only briefly; Trish was overwhelmed with the news, and after we hung up she began reading the news reports. She read them late into the night, each terrible detail, and when her husband came home from his trucking job, she sat him down to tell him what happened in person.

"His words was, 'Let's go get the kids,'" Trish told me the next day, sounding dazed and exhausted. "I looked at him and realized, this isn't sinking in. He's in shock. I said, 'John, they're gone,' and he said, 'What? Where do we pick up Hannah?' I said, 'Baby, we're not picking anybody up.' He has a denial, you know?"

Since Trish and John were estranged from Tammy, Trish had to track down a working phone number. When she called her stepdaughter the next day with the news, Tammy became hysterical.

Many reporters feel that delivering news about a person's death to family members or friends of that person is their worst nightmare. It often happens by accident—police don't usually talk to the media at the beginning of an investigation, and so breaking news reporters who are knocking on doors may assume the cops have gotten there first when they haven't. Some reporters who have delivered news of a death to family or friends feel racked with guilt for years afterward. Journalists aren't trained to deliver this kind of news, and witnessing people's immediate grief firsthand can be overwhelming. The grief is also often coupled with anger from family members, who feel disrespected to learn such life-shattering news in such an undignified way.

When I set out to find Tammy that fall, I presumed she was already aware of what had happened to her children. It was true that, back in May, the Mendocino County Sheriff's Office had made a public appeal for the family of Markis, Hannah, and Abigail to come forward, because they needed DNA to test against Hannah's partial remains. But the records containing the children's birth names were in the investigative files released by the police. The police, who had these names before any journalists did, made these files public. Moreover, the death of her children was national news, broadcast on CNN, splashed across *The New York Times* and *The Washington Post*, and shared throughout Twitter and Facebook. Millions of people had heard about the event in the six months since it had happened, and had pored over graphic details of the abuse and murder of her children. When Trish responded to my Facebook message, I was floored when I realized she didn't know. But then I remembered what Sherry had said—no one had called her, either; if her family's lawyer hadn't found out, she probably never would have known.

"I'm devastated, the news I've been reading and everything, it's crushing to me, and I'm trying to process all of this, and trying to still live my life," Tammy said when she called, the day after Trish had told her that her children were dead. "Because I'm at a point where I don't even want to live behind this."

Tammy had been deeply depressed by the removal and adoption of her children more than a decade prior—grieving them, she said, as if they were dead. But she'd maintained hope that, once they were old enough, she would see them again, tell them she loved them, and explain to them what led to her removal from their lives. That hope had now been snatched from her, brutally. A precarious support system that she'd been trying to build ever since began to crumble.

She'd moved from Houston to Mobile, Alabama, just a month before she found out, and things had already been pretty tense. She was living with the family of her husband, Rob, and they didn't seem to like her much, she thought. She and Rob were paying his mother rent to live in a bedroom in the mother's home, and their arguments were frequent.

Typically, a journalist's job is to get the breaking news out as soon as possible. In this case, no one—including the law enforcement agencies investigating the case—yet knew the identity of the Harts' first adoptive children's birth mother; surely this was an important discovery. But I quickly realized in my early talks with Tammy that her mental health was at a crisis point and that she needed help urgently. She had told me multiple times in those first calls that she wanted to end her life. She'd also shared that she had several serious mental illness diagnoses.

I had never been in this situation as a journalist, but it was clear that Tammy was not ready to have a story come out identifying her by name. In the meantime, I reached out to a nonprofit that had emailed me previously to share that it provides no-cost therapy for birth mothers. The organization got to work finding a therapist in Mobile who would accept payment from them for assisting Tammy.

Tammy did go to see the therapist a couple of times, but she had to take the bus across town to do it, which was unreliable, and after a few sessions, she stopped going. Plus, she said, she'd spent her whole childhood talking to therapists, and she could tell them what they were about to say before they said it. None of it helped anyway, she said.

Tammy's first priority was to submit a DNA sample so that the California police could identify Hannah. She called

the Mendocino County Sheriff's Office right away, identified
herself as Markis, Hannah, and Abigail's mother, and offered
to submit her DNA to test against the remains of the foot
found on the beach. The Mendocino sheriff contacted the
Mobile Police Department, which sent an officer to collect
a swab from Tammy and send the sample to a U.S. Department of Justice lab.

While Tammy waited for the results of that test, we began to speak frequently by phone. Tammy told me she was
scared of what the scrutiny of the news media would bring
to her life, and worried about the effect it would have on her
relationship with Rob. The news about her children had sent
her life, already in a precarious balance, into a total whirl-
wind, threatening to pin her down for good under the weight
of her grief. Her marriage, which was volatile in the best of
times, had taken an even more brutal turn. She wasn't allowed to speak about the children in the home she shared
with Rob's family. Rob had told her that she was not to tell
his family the full story of how she lost her children.

Tammy would wait for Rob to leave the house and
then call me to share snippets of background, interspersing
her conversation with accounts of the crisis she found herself
in currently, overcome with grief and in a hostile environment. Once during a call, her husband came home, and they
began to argue before she abruptly hung up.

A week later, she called from a domestic violence shelter.
She told me that Rob had beat her up, not for the first time.
After he threw her against a wall during an argument, she

had looked around to find a shelter that would let her bring her tiny old Yorkie, Toto, along with her.

Tammy lived on her disability check, which was about $600 a month, and so leaving Rob was a lot harder than just making a choice—and the choice itself, after six years of ups and downs, was hard enough. On January 3, 2019, her birthday, she took an overdose of the insulin shot she gave herself daily to manage her diabetes, hoping to end her life. But she woke up the next day, thinking God had intervened. "As many times as I have tried to kill myself and it hasn't worked, he must have other plans for me," she said.

A week after Tammy attempted suicide, the results of the DNA test came back. A woman in the Mendocino Sheriff's Office reached out to Tammy by email, asking for her to call. But just hours later, before Tammy had even checked her email, Lieutenant Shannon Barney sent out a press release to the national media following the case, positively identifying Hannah's body based on Tammy's DNA sample. The story hit the news; I texted Tammy a screenshot when I saw it. Tammy was livid, and hurt. "Why didn't they call me?" she asked. "When I signed my rights over, my right to know anything went away."

She called the sheriff's office, upset. Could she at least have the remains of Hannah that they'd identified? It wasn't possible, she was told. They'd have to go to the next of kin, which in this case were the parents of Jennifer and Sarah. Could the sheriff's office tell Jennifer and Sarah's family, at least, that Tammy had the desire to have her children's remains back with her? They'd see what they could do, they told her. She never heard from them again.

As far as the law is concerned, law enforcement did nothing wrong in failing to notify Tammy Scheurich and Sherry Davis of the deaths of their children. "I don't know of any law that requires anything like that once your rights have been terminated to a child," said Vivek Sankaran, a child welfare reform advocate and law professor at the University of Michigan Law School. Sankaran said he was in a similar situation with a client he was representing in her appeal of her parental termination case in the law clinic at the university. Her child, who had significant medical needs, died while in foster care. Sankaran learned this when the state's attorney called to tell him that the appeal he filed was moot. He had to tell his client and her family the news. "It was one of the worst moments of my career," Sankaran said. "It was just really infuriating to me that nobody had picked up the phone and passed that information on in a more humane way."

Judges and attorneys representing the state, Sankaran said, rarely consider the emotional impact of the life-altering decisions that happen in family court—both on the parents and the children themselves. "The number one thing that bothers me about how we conduct business in foster care is that we've lost key concepts like humanity, dignity," he said. "We're prioritizing compliance and the needs of bureaucracy."

Suzanne Sellers is the executive director of the nonprofit Families Organizing for Child Welfare Justice. In 1999, she lost the rights to her two children, who were subsequently adopted; her children each got in touch with her when they turned eighteen. Sellers still grieves being out of contact with her children for so many years, when she wasn't allowed to have a hand in parenting them or to even know how they were doing. "Once adopted, the law says that . . . all of the rights and care transfers to the adopted parents, and the mothers—the birth mothers—are expected to just disappear, just go away," Sellers said. "And that's very difficult to do, emotionally, spiritually, physically. We still do exist."

13

"Something I Could Love Unconditionally"

As far back as Tammy can remember, she had always wanted a baby. As a young child, she had baby dolls, and she treated them like they were real. Her grandmother, whom she called Mom, bought her a Baby Alive doll, which moved its mouth and head, drank from a bottle, and even made a mess of its diaper. Tammy wanted real baby bottles for her baby, though—the kind with little disposable bags inside—and she asked for real diapers at the grocery store. She pushed her baby around in a classic full-sized pram—a gift from Mom and Papa, her grandfather.

Mom and Papa were happy to oblige. Tammy had been living with them most of her life in Ingleside, Texas, after being separated from her mother, Maxina, as a toddler. Her father, John, was in the military, and he lived with Tammy and Mom and Papa when he wasn't on base. When Tammy was three or four, she began splitting her time between Maxina's house and her grandparents', and her caregivers began to notice alarming behavior. Tammy was acting out sexually at bath time, and once tried to stick her hand down Maxina's new husband's pants. The family came to believe she had likely been abused.

Tammy says she remembers her father's sexual abuse, and that it happened early in her life. His wife, Trish, who is Tammy's stepmother, denies that it happened and says that Tammy had previously retracted claims she'd made about the abuse. "Tammy's not a victim," Trish said. (John recently had a stroke, can't communicate well, and declined to be interviewed. Tammy's grandparents are dead.)

But Tammy says her father moved out at this time, and she continued to live with her grandparents. Tammy's grandfather was a minister at the Ingleside Church of Christ, but he never reported the alleged sexual abuse. Tammy says that her grandmother apologized to her for that when Tammy took care of her while she was dying.

From the outside, things at home were fairly perfect—Tammy wore pretty dresses, with matching hair accessories, and her grandparents doted on her. Her grandmother volunteered as a class mom at her school. But Tammy had had strong sexual urges from a very young age, and she began acting out with other children. By the time she got her first period at age eleven, she was no longer a virgin, having had sex behind a dumpster with a thirteen-year-old deaf boy while on a visit to her aunt and uncle's in Columbus, Texas.

Though they'd seen her act out, her grandparents didn't know about her sexual behavior outside the home. The Church of Christ is a group of fundamentalist churches, each independent. They are known for disallowing the use of instruments in church; members believe that traditional a cappella renditions of gospel songs are how God intended them to be sung. While Tammy's maternal instincts were strongly encouraged, premarital sex was blasphemous and unacceptable.

But for Tammy, the distinction was not so sharp. She started having sex at age eleven in part so that she could get pregnant. "I just figured, if I could be a momma, there had to be something I could love unconditionally, that they would love me unconditionally, and the world would be beautiful," she said.

As she hit puberty, her sexual feelings increased alongside intrusive thoughts and terrifying feelings of being abandoned. She began to seek out boys and even men, and her grandparents, once so focused on providing her love and attention and clothes and toys, began to back off from her. In their three-bedroom house, what was once her playroom next to her room became her grandfather's office. Her grandmother stopped volunteering to be class mom. And Tammy, feeling rejected, became more and more urgently insistent on getting a man's attention.

She began to frequent "party lines," call-in numbers through which strangers would talk over each other in a group and find interested parties to pair off with in one-on-one chat rooms. She talked all night on the phone with guys of indeterminate ages, until her grandfather got a thousand-dollar phone bill from charges to the Dominican Republic. He was livid, which only reinforced Tammy's desire to seek attention and care outside of her family.

When she was thirteen, Tammy threatened to attempt suicide and was sent to the San Antonio State Hospital. This was the first of three back-to-back stays there for threats or attempts of suicide. "Their solution for everything at the state hospital is medicine—get 'em doped up, you know? I mean, people walking around there drooling, it's like a really traumatic kind of thing," she says. Her last stint there was six months, while she waited for a bed at the Waco Center for Youth, another state-run psychiatric hospital, this one for thirteen- to seventeen-year-olds who had "exhausted available community treatment resources."

Waco Center for Youth took the opposite approach to medicine from the San Antonio hospital. Tammy went cold turkey off her meds. "I was just a mess," she says. During her institutionalization, Tammy was diagnosed with borderline personality disorder, bipolar disorder, PTSD, and major depression.

Borderline personality disorder is characterized by a crippling fear of abandonment, unstable relationships, impulsive behavior, self-harm, and difficulty regulating emotions. Researchers have linked BPD to childhood sexual abuse, and people with BPD are more likely than the general population to have PTSD, too. Tammy says now that she clearly sees her suicide attempts as bids for attention from her family, and her sexual behavior as an effort to create bonds with people who wouldn't leave her. But her struggle to form connections only ended with her family and partners pushing her away.

Her father, during this time, started a relationship with Trish, who was then seventeen. Trish was just a few years older than Tammy, and Tammy was threatened by her. She felt that her dad's attention, which was already divided between her and his two younger sons from his second marriage, was even more limited now that Trish was in the picture. When her father and Mom and Papa drove her to the Waco Center for Youth, they were supposed to stay in the center's family cottage for the weekend while Tammy settled in. But Trish called to say she had been in a car accident, so her father and grandparents had to head back right after they dropped her off. Tammy would be in the Waco Center for Youth, hours away from her family, for thirteen months.

Throughout her time in the two state hospitals, she had maintained a relationship with a man named Mark whom she had met on the party line when she was thirteen. He lived in California. He'd sent her pictures of himself—he was part Samoan, with shiny black hair, and in his twenties. Tammy snuck to call him from the pay phone at the group home, and when she got back to her grandparents' house from Waco, he sent her money to buy a plane ticket to come and see him.

She was sixteen then, and without telling her grandparents, she flew out to California just before Valentine's Day. At the airport, she didn't recognize Mark. He was significantly older than his photo suggested, with streaks of gray in his hair, and much heavier, too. He booked a motel room for them, but Tammy was too scared to sleep there with him.

Instead, she sat in the lobby; the man behind the counter gave her a box of Valentine's chocolates and kept an eye on her all night. The next day, Mark drove her to the airport and she went home.

She was miserable back at her grandparents'. She tried to avoid school any way she could. She hadn't learned much of anything at the two institutions, which had all the kids grouped together in one class, despite their age differences. They were teaching her basic addition and subtraction, even though she was beginning to learn algebra back at home. When she started back at school in Ingleside, she was nearly two years behind her peers, who made fun of her for being chubby and for being in special education classes. She hated it; she had no friends. She decided to quit.

She got back in touch with her mother, Maxina, and on a Greyhound bus out to Georgia to see her for the first time in years, she met another much older man. When she turned seventeen, she took the bus into Houston in order to link up with him. But when she arrived in the city, he stood her up. "You made your bed, you lie in it," her grandfather told her when she called him from the station. "That was my lesson, and that's how I became homeless," Tammy said. She stayed in and around the Houston Greyhound station for a month before her grandparents allowed her to come back home.

Shortly after coming to Houston the first time, Tammy began a relationship with a Black man named Mark and got pregnant with Markis, who was born when Tammy was eighteen. As Tammy moved between Houston and Corpus, spending stretches of time on the streets, Markis stayed mostly with Mom and Papa. Mom and Papa were getting on in years, and Markis kept them young; Papa brought Markis along everywhere he went, and Markis loved to ride around with him as they ran errands in his truck.

Markis was a live wire, his family recalled. He was diagnosed with ADHD, and took medication for it. When he was three and a half, his little sister Hannah was born, to a different father, also a Black man. Things had calmed down a bit by then, Tammy recalls, and she mostly stayed with her children at her grandparents' house or with John and Trish in Ingleside, across the bay from Corpus in San Patricio County.

That's where she was, pregnant with Abigail, when a series of events led to her entanglement with CPS. At a birthday party for Markis in July 2003, Hannah, then one and a half, got covered with ant bites. When people noticed her screaming, Tammy dunked her in a kiddie pool to wash off the ants. Later, one of the bites got infected with a hard-to-treat staph infection, MRSA. "They had to remove a chunk the size of a quarter, and that deep, and gave her IV antibiotics," Tammy says.

A doctor informed CPS, which opened a case for potential medical neglect. "Here in San Patricio County, I vouched for Tammy, because it wasn't Tammy's fault," Trish says. "As soon as Hannah started screaming and yelling, Tammy addressed the problem and did what she could. She got bit. She sought treatment for this."

But CPS's involvement scared Tammy, and made her question her ability to parent. She'd gotten pregnant a third time from a brief fling with another man. She initially decided early on to place the baby, who was not yet born, for adoption. "I remember having an ultrasound and not wanting to look at the screen," she said.

But Tammy moved, along with her grandparents, to Columbus, a small town west of Houston, where Tammy's aunt and uncle lived. Tammy reconsidered letting her next child go. "Things had calmed down so much and I could see light at the end of the tunnel, and I thought, 'Yes, I could do this.'" Abigail was born the day after Christmas in 2003. Less than two months later, Tammy would lose custody of her children for good.

It was February 2004, and the air in Columbus was cool and damp, even as flowers were starting to bloom. It was just weeks before Hannah's second birthday, and she had an upper respiratory infection that had turned into pneumonia.

Tammy said she had taken Hannah to the doctor in Columbus on February 9, and the doctor had changed Hannah's asthma medications and sent them home. But according to a police report filed the next month, Tammy did not show for a planned doctor's appointment the next day and waited too long to take Hannah to a hospital, as instructed by a doctor over the phone. Columbus was a town of about three thousand, and Tammy didn't trust the local hospital; she said a nurse there had accidentally sneezed while giving Hannah a steroid shot for her asthma one time and jabbed the child with the needle. Tammy wanted Hannah to go to Texas Children's, an hour away in Houston, a world-class hospital in the

Texas Medical Center. Tammy didn't have a car, and Mom and Papa were on a day trip to Austin. There was no one to watch Markis when he got home from school or to care for baby Abigail. When Tammy called an ambulance, they told her they were unable to transport Abigail or Markis along with them. With no one to care for her other two children, she was forced to wait for a ride.

That ride was her caseworker, Sharon Kearbey. Tammy remembers what was happening when Sharon knocked on her door. She had just changed Abigail's diaper, and set the dirty one on the nightstand, putting the baby back in her bassinet next to her own bed. Hannah was burning up with a fever, talking gibberish, and Tammy was trying to calm her on the bed. On the TV, *Finding Nemo*, Markis's favorite movie, was playing. The bus had just dropped him off from school.

Markis answered the door. "Sharon was standing there in my living room," Tammy recalled. She had been scared to call Sharon, because she didn't want it to look bad for her case, she says. "She reassured me she wasn't taking the kids away and that CPS was there to help in other ways."

At the hospital, though, things took a different tone. Markis hadn't taken his ADHD medicine that day, Tammy remembers, and he was bouncing off the walls, sometimes leaving the room and wandering down the hall. She could tell the nurses were bothered by it, but with Hannah so sick and Abigail just two weeks old, Tammy had her hands full. After a while, a nurse came in and asked to speak to Sharon, the caseworker. When Sharon came back into the room, she told Tammy that CPS was removing her children. "She already had the paperwork in her hand," Tammy said, crying.

There's a close relationship between hospitals and child welfare agencies. In cases of child abuse, teams of pediatricians judge how children likely came to be injured. They also assess cases of medical neglect, in which parents may be found not to have attained needed medical care for their children. Hospitals, and particularly public hospitals, are a key entry point into the child welfare system in another way: They choose which mothers get drug tested at the birth of their children, and if those tests are positive, they can report the mothers, at least in Texas, for physical abuse. Tammy felt blindsided by the neglect charge, because she had been working to get a ride for her family to the hospital. The open CPS case over Hannah's staph infection in Nueces County likely influenced the doctor's determination that her delay in getting Hannah to the hospital constituted medical neglect.

Colorado County not only removed Tammy's children but also charged her with child endangerment. The indictment says that she did "intentionally, knowingly, recklessly, or with criminal negligence, engage in conduct, by omission, that placed Hannah Holliday-Scheurich, a child younger than 15 years of age, in imminent danger of death, bodily injury, or physical or mental impairment, by failing to seek medical treatment for her."

Tammy was originally given three years of "deferred adjudication," which is similar to probation, but after she failed to pay the monthly court fees totaling $225 and missed assigned community service, she was given thirty days in jail in

April 2005. After she got out, she again failed to follow court orders, which included paying $1,266 in fees, and was sentenced to another six months in jail on December 19, 2006.

Tammy was on a fixed income of just over $600 a month from her disability benefits; she said she didn't have any extra money to pay the fees. "I just didn't follow through with my probation stuff . . . I'd go and report for my probation visits, but as far as paying anything, I didn't pay anything," Scheurich said. "I didn't have the money to pay."

The relationship between an inability to pay fines and incarceration is well documented. Many jurisdictions around the country rely on punitive fines and additional court fees to help fund their court systems. It's largely ineffective, as an analysis by New York University's Brennan Center for Justice found, because the cost of jailing those unable to pay is so exorbitant. It also leads to jailing people for being poor; middle-class people can pay fines and fees easily, while to those who are on a fixed income, like Tammy, $225, let alone $1,266, is an amount that's impossible to raise.

Jail was traumatizing for her. Tammy hadn't had much criminal involvement, besides a couple of minor infractions, and to her, there was no greater punishment than the loss of her children. Although she had an extensive documented history of mental health issues, and was and is receiving federal disability benefits because of them, Tammy was not offered any mental health support during her CPS investigation or the subsequent relinquishment of her rights. She lost confidence that she could be a good parent; her abandonment issues intensified.

Qualitative research has shown that parents with borderline personality disorder struggle to manage their mental health and to simultaneously be the parents they want to be. A 2020 study of twelve parents and twenty-one practitioners who served them, published in *Frontiers of Psychology*, found that parents with BPD sometimes experience emotions so intensely that it becomes hard to attune to the emotions of their children. "Many of the parents described childhoods lacking nurture and love or characterized by anger and violence. Some experienced abuse in childhood or adolescence, often perpetrated by individuals within their family. For parents, their experience of being a parent was directly related to the maladaptive parenting they had experienced, to traumatic early life experiences, or both," the researchers wrote. The study's participants said they were largely unable to access support in parenting, and for those to whom support was offered, many were afraid to accept it. "This was often rooted in a fear of child-removal," the study's authors wrote.

The first time Tammy was involved with CPS in Ingleside, she'd completed all her parenting classes and the rest of the stipulations of her service plan. But with her children gone, what use was there to follow through on community service? When Tammy lost her children, she entered a deep depression. Normally a clean freak, Tammy couldn't get herself out of bed to take a shower or to take out the trash. The dishes that were in the sink when she'd gone to the hospital stayed there so long that maggots grew on them and turned to flies. The shades stayed drawn all day and night, and *Finding Nemo* played on a loop on the bedroom television. Tammy lay in bed for days, watching Marlin, the worried father fish, traverse the ocean, searching desperately for his lost son.

After that day in the hospital with Hannah, Tammy would never again have custody of her children. Months later, she voluntarily signed away her rights, expecting that the kids would be placed with the foster family they had been living with in Missouri City, a suburb of Houston. She was in touch with the couple who was fostering them, and they assured Tammy that she would be able to stay in their lives. But later she found out through CPS that the adoption fell through. The kids were adopted out of state instead.

Very few details of the foster family exist—the children's case files aren't available, and neither Tammy nor her caseworker can remember the family's name. Because Texas seals all its CPS and adoption records, it's unclear why the initial placement fell through. Tammy remembers the family as a Black couple with three children of their own. She thought they would provide a good home for her children, all three of whom were biracial. They even took the kids to Disney World, she remembers. "I had talked to the foster mom and had everything mapped out in my head, how it was going to be," she said. "And it didn't happen that way."

Tammy holds a special, heated grudge—a passionate hate, actually—for her caseworker, Sharon Kearbey. She'd trusted Sharon, gotten close with her. She remembers Sharon taking her out to eat, and once stopping at a Ross to help Sharon pick out a suitcase. She now feels manipulated, lied to, and coerced into relinquishing her rights based on what she now sees as incorrect information. She didn't know her kids would be sent so far away; she didn't know she wouldn't be able to see them or get updates on their lives, as she'd worked out with their foster mother. And she sure as hell would never in a million years have fathomed that they'd be sent somewhere to be abused. Tammy read in news stories that Markis and Hannah seemed to get the worst of Jennifer's rage. *Why?* She wondered. *Why was Hannah so small?* When she first saw their photos in the news stories, she thought Hannah must have been Abigail. "She was never small like that," she says. She has hatred for Jennifer and Sarah, sure, but they are already dead. It's Sharon, she thinks, who really deserves to suffer.

Sharon Kearbey is no longer with the agency; she goes by a different last name now, but asked that I don't identify it. She said Tammy had a pattern of neglecting to seek medical care for her children, and that Tammy should have called her earlier to take Hannah to the hospital. She doesn't remember the names of the kids' foster parents either, but she vaguely remembers that the couple was having marital problems, and that they decided they couldn't care for all of the children.

Trish and John wanted Markis, Sharon remembers, but Trish had recently broken her back and was worried about how she could take care of a toddler and a newborn. "I did everything I could for those kids," Sharon said in a Facebook message to me. "I loved them." Her priority, she says, was to place the siblings in one home. "We try to do everything we can to keep them together," she added. "It's hard enough to lose your parents/family but to lose your siblings and never know where they went is worse."

When Jennifer and Sarah Hart saw the children on the Texas Adoption Resource Exchange website, they reached out and were put in touch with Sharon. They spoke by phone, and she took to the couple immediately. On Abigail's second birthday, the day after Christmas 2005, Jennifer and Sarah came down to Houston to meet Markis, Hannah, and Abigail at their foster home, the first step in deciding if the children would be a good fit. This meeting is when Jennifer first held baby Abigail, later posting on her Facebook that she instantly fell in love. The Harts still had their foster daughter, Brie, at home, but by March 2006, Brie had been sent packing and the Harts moved their new kids to Minnesota. By September that year, the children were formally adopted. Sharon says she spoke with the children after the adoption. "They never disclosed anything to me," she said. "I had a great relationship with the kids before they were adopted so I felt like they would have told me if something was wrong."

In February 2007, Jennifer sent Sharon an email, telling her that "a little birdie" told her that Sharon would be in South Dakota and suggesting they meet up. Sharon said she had to wait to book her trip because she was waiting on a review for another family from the Interstate Compact on the Placement of Children—the same process the Harts had gone through.

"Oh, and Markis just came back from his FINAL Dr. Spaulding (med doctor) visit today . . . since he has been off meds completely since Nov," Jen responded. "Dr. said he didn't need to come back anymore since he is doing so well. He wanted you to know."

Sharon did end up visiting the children in Minnesota after they were adopted, in an unofficial capacity, she told me, and it was Markis who had convinced her that the kids were really happy with the Harts. "Markis was a very withdrawn child when we took him into care. He did not open up until he had been with the Harts for a while," she says. "It was one of the things that gave me a good feeling about them. He was withdrawn even in the foster home before them, but once he was there he opened up, was talkative, and more expressive."

When she heard about what happened to the family, she cried for days—even though she didn't believe, at first, that Jennifer had deliberately driven off the cliff.

"I thought they had it wrong and it must have been an accident. Honestly, I'm not sure I still don't believe that [it] wasn't," she told me in 2021.

I asked her if she had read detailed accounts of what had happened to the family. She said she hadn't. I asked her if she had any thoughts about what might have happened.

"I don't," she said. "No one can predict the future, and I can only assume something happened that caused such a drastic change."

Trish Scheurich says that she and John wanted to take Markis, Hannah, and Abigail when they were removed from Tammy. Yet for some reason, she says, Sharon would not do a home study on them, the first necessary step in order to place children with their relatives. Trish supposes it might have been because she'd recently broken her back at that time, and had a limited capacity to provide care. Reports of John's alleged abuse of Tammy as a child did not reach Sharon and thus played no role in her decision.

After she lost Markis, Hannah, and Abigail, Tammy had two more children. Alex (not his real name) was born in 2006, and John and Trish took custody of him, without CPS initiating a court case, when he was two months old. Tammy had been precariously housed, and had Alex while living in a motel. Baby John was born in 2008, five weeks early, and although her father was with her in the hospital when she gave birth, and she named her youngest son after him, she chose to place him in an adoptive home rather than give her father and stepmother custody.

The relationship between Tammy and her father was always rocky, but in this period it became volatile. She thought that her family's behavior was, at times, racist, and she resented their front-and-center role with her children. After Baby John was born, he was put in the neonatal intensive care unit, and the hospital communicated with Tammy's father, John, directly, bypassing Tammy herself, she says.

By the time Baby John came around, Tammy had found an institution she trusted. Kim and Martin Dale ran a "street church," a weekly pop-up of sorts; it was located just behind the main drag in Montrose, Houston's gay neighborhood, which acted as a magnet for the city's young homeless people. They'd preach to the street kids while feeding them dinner, and through this weekly event, Tammy came to know Kim well. She decided to arrange for Baby John's adoption to a family Kim knew in the Houston area. This caused a major rift between Tammy and her father and stepmother, who never quite forgave her.

"When I lost my kids, I lost my direction. I didn't have anything grounding me anymore," Tammy says of her first three children. "I couldn't even bond properly with them when I had my [last two] children because I was so scared they were gonna get taken away for some reason or another."

As for Alex, he began to act out violently at around five or six, which only worsened when, in the midst of a blow-up fight with Trish, Tammy told Alex that she was his real mother. Up until that point, Alex had thought he was the child of Trish and John. Increasing acts of violence against other children and animals in the home, Trish said, led them to have Alex placed in an institutional treatment facility, where he has been for years.

John and Trish stopped speaking to Tammy after that fight. Over the years, she would sometimes call, always from different numbers, Trish said, but the couple stopped wanting to have anything to do with her. Things couldn't get much worse between them, but they were all badly shaken by the news of the three oldest children's deaths. Trish took to bed and stayed there for several days. She tortured herself reading every single account she could find of the heinous crimes committed against her grandchildren. "I said, 'You know, Tammy, I blame you and I blame CPS, but I also blame us,'" she told me from bed days later. "It's hard to accept that you failed. And child protection failed. I was looking at my granddaughter yesterday, and she favors Hannah. What could I have done more, better?"

Her mind kept returning to the last time she saw Markis. They were at Papa's house, and she was sitting at the kitchen table with him while he had some cookies and milk. He asked for more milk, and as Trish got up to get it for him, his cup, with some milk still in it, knocked over and spilled out. "Uh-oh!" he said, looking at Trish to gauge her reaction.

"I told him, 'That's okay, messes are meant to be made,'" she remembers. Markis smiled, and dipped his cookie into the puddle of milk on the table. "Fixed it!" he said with a big smile.

She reached over the puddle of milk on the table, poured more milk in his cup, and grabbed a cookie for herself. "Those are my memories," she said, "and they're all I have."

While Tammy was at the women's shelter in Mobile, she joined several of the Facebook groups that had sprung up in the wake of the crash. Those sites often focused on theories about the children who remained missing and the psychological motives of the Hart women. Tammy mostly joined the groups to screenshot photos of her children, marveling at how they'd changed in the time since she'd last seen them. At first she kept silent, but then she decided to reach out to one of the moderators. They became friends of a sort, and when the woman heard of Tammy's plight in Mobile, she posted to the group about her situation, asking for donations to help Tammy leave town. But later, Tammy and the Facebook group monitor would fall out. The woman would tell the group that she thought Tammy lied about being suicidal and took advantage of her kindness to get donations. "What I am struggling with is that she used the compassionate hearts of all of you," she wrote in a long group post.

Tammy maintained that she showed the woman receipts for the luggage and the bus ticket, and that she hadn't lied about anything. But the situation was complicated by the fact that she had also fallen out with the friend she had been staying with in Houston. That friend, Michell Reedy, had picked Tammy up from the Greyhound station and taken her back to stay at the apartment that she shared with her adult son. Tammy brought along her Yorkie, Toto, who came with her everywhere she went. She cleaned the apartment and cooked meals to express her gratitude for the place to stay. But as the situation soured with Michell and her son, Michell reached out to the Facebook moderator to complain about Tammy, whose problems had spiraled. Soon, she'd be on the move again. Not long before that happened, I went to see Tammy at Michell's apartment in northeast Houston. She sat at the dining table, chain-smoking and blowing the smoke through the open sliding-glass door and out to the balcony. It had been four months since I found her, and since she learned that her children had been killed. We were finally meeting in person for the first time.

Tammy has a weather-worn reddish-tan face and a bumblebee tattoo on her cheek up near her right eye. Her eyes are a piercing blue-green, and her smoky voice is peppered with

Texanisms. The air coming in from the balcony was chilly. It was February, and she'd just gotten back to Houston.

Usually, missing front teeth in an adult causes a speech impediment. Tammy's voice, however, is smooth and husky; she has just the tiniest hint of a lisp, which is mostly masked by her drawl. Her natural underbite showed her bottom teeth instead of her top row, which made the missing ones almost imperceptible. "These two and this one are out," she says, pointing to the empty space in her mouth, "and these two are broke off at the gum."

Tammy explains that a fight with her husband, Rob, is responsible for the loss of her teeth. "He knocked one of my teeth out in the front, and I had to go get another one pulled out. Because he had hit me so hard," Tammy recalls. "I told Rob, 'Why don't we get this one taken out to the side, and then we'll just tie a string around this one and slam a door or something,' which I'm glad I didn't." She pauses to blow smoke out the back door.

She'd left Rob before, and she'd even stayed with Michell before while broken up with Rob, but she'd always gone back, usually days later. Not this time, she told me. She felt fully healed. He was calling her, she admitted, even as we sat there talking. But this time, she was moving on.

Tammy and Rob had gotten together after Baby John was born. Rob was a military man, like her father, and as a result, he managed PTSD, along with several other serious mental health diagnoses. When they met, Rob was living in a single-room apartment in a complex designated for low-income or homeless veterans on the edge of Houston's Montrose neighborhood. They had both been homeless on and off through the years. She says she never developed a drug habit, and adds that she always felt accepted among her peers on the street in a way she never felt in her "real" life. "The streets have been one of those places that I always kind of turn to, because the people out there don't look down on you," she said. "It's almost like a family, if you think of it like that, and you don't get judged. Everyone has a story."

The violence was intermittent, not constant, and that's what made it hard to quit. Rob could be charming, sweet. He understood the things she'd been through, as he'd been through a lot himself. But his anger could turn on a dime, and especially when he was drinking, he could be violent, hurtful, and mean.

Tammy could lash out herself. That was something she was quick to say, and it ended up softening his abuse in her eyes. If she left Rob for good, then she was really alone in the world—no family, no one to love her. Her worst fear, and the thing she spent her entire life trying to avoid.

She was adrift, again, like she'd been after her children were first removed from her care. Her family didn't want to rekindle their relationship, and her friendships were splintering. She'd be back in Mobile with Rob by spring.

14

"Death at the Hands of Another"

The investigation into the Harts' fatal plunge involved an intricate web of law enforcement and social service agencies, spanning the states where the family lived. But Mendocino County is where the family died, and the sheriff's office there had taken the lead in notifying the public of developments in the case. At regular intervals since the crash, the department had been speaking to the public and putting out press releases; the news they announced regarding the identification of Hannah—before Tammy was notified herself—was in one of these releases.

Mendocino County sheriff Tom Allman was the public face of the investigation. A law enforcement lifer, with more than thirty years rising in the ranks in various departments around California, and even a brief term as a United Nations blue beret in Kosovo, Allman clearly loved holding the microphone in a high-profile case. He said the deaths of the Hart family constituted the "largest mass murder in our county in modern times."

In early 2019, Allman told a reporter that he was convening a public inquest into the deaths of the Harts. It was clear from Allman's interview that the inquest was to be a finale of sorts to the case. He told the reporter that the evidence his office had collected would likely "shock the consciousness" of those who had been following along.

"This is the first coroner's inquest we've had in this county in at least 50 years, that I know of," he said. Inquests in major cases are rare these days, so much so that Allman felt the need to explain the procedure to the press. Typically led by a coroner, the practice began centuries ago in England to help ascertain a cause of death in a suspicious or sudden case. An inquest is not a criminal case, so there are no convictions; rather, a jury gathers to hear the evidence unearthed in the investigation and makes a ruling as to the cause of death. It's not adversarial and therefore the rules are looser: witnesses are allowed to testify to hearsay, or things they did not experience directly, and there's no cross-examination of the witnesses. In a case like that of the Harts, which was suspicious and had generated a lot of interest but in which there were no survivors, it was, Allman said, the closest thing to a final legal result.

"And it will be the result of one of three things: One, a terrible accident; two, a homicidal driver," Allman said, "or three, a 'Thelma and Louise' situation where two mothers felt that the pressures of life had gotten too great, and they decided to take their own lives and the lives of their children."

Thelma & Louise, the 1991 movie starring Susan Sarandon and Geena Davis, is about two friends on a road trip who end up killing a man after he attacks one of them in an attempted rape. Regarded as a feminist classic, the film ends when the two women hold hands and drive their sparkly blue Thunderbird convertible off a cliff, rather than be apprehended by the police.

There are no children in the backseat in *Thelma & Louise*. The movie's final scene depicts a suicide, not a murder. Allman's allusion to the movie was more in line with Jennifer's understanding of herself as an unfairly hounded mother than with the actual facts of the case. The police narrative, it seemed, was one of two well-meaning women who succumbed to great outside pressures, driving them to end their family's lives. That narrative would be one of several reactions the family's death provoked in the viral responses to the case.

In some ways, this was the perfect tabloid crime—innocent children, mean mommies, harrowing and unusual deaths. True crime aficionados were especially drawn to the case by the underlying psychological question, *What kind of woman could do this to her family?*

The Hart family's story got the true crime treatment before the inquest even took place: *Glamour* magazine, in conjunction with the website HowStuffWorks, released an eight-part podcast, "Broken Harts," delving into the Hart family's life and particularly focusing on Jennifer.

"I am a mother of a two-year-old. I can't imagine ever being pushed to the brink that way, but at the same time, it is a relatable feeling as a mother, as a woman, to feel trapped by the choices you make," the podcast host Justine Harman says in the first episode.

In a later episode, Harman does a thought experiment, again involving her young child: "Sometimes, when I tuck my two-year-old in at night . . . he gives me this look like, 'I'm going to get out of this bed.' And I give him another one that says, 'Don't you dare.' And he doesn't. He doesn't dare," Harman says. "What a strange influence to have over another person, but what if I pushed it a little further? What if I told him that something bad would happen to him if he got out of bed? What if, and this is honestly hard for me to say out loud, what if I held him down until it hurt?"

The podcast asks listeners to empathize—but with whom? "Broken Harts" includes very little information about the children's birth families, and no information at all about the children's mothers, Sherry Davis and Tammy Scheurich, other than to note that Sherry is a cocaine user. But it does ask the listener to imagine what it might feel like to hurt their own child.

True crime and stressed parent themes were not the only ones to circulate. The case touched a nerve for some trans-racial adoptees, who saw the tension between the children's performance of happiness and the brutal treatment described in the abuse allegations made against the mothers. Black people, and especially Black mothers, saw the racism steeped into the interactions between the children and those who could help them, and the self-congratulatory tone of Jennifer's public persona was particularly grating to them.

The myriad Facebook groups that popped up, like the ones Tammy joined, typified the range of responses to the story. The groups had thousands of members, and they shared theories and questions about minute details of the case. But exchanges quickly became heated as opinions clashed. Black women in the group highlighting the racism the children experienced were sometimes silenced, with their posts being removed, and their ability to comment on some controversial posts getting turned off by moderators.

After I wrote my first story about Sherry Davis and Clarence Celestine, in April 2018, people in some of the groups found Sherry's Facebook profile and started posting screenshots of her page that showed her daily life in Southlawn. Many of the posts showed her in a negative light. "Looks like she would have made a fabulous mom," one woman commented sarcastically after posting the screenshots.

Some posters pushed back, calling the doxxing of Sherry racist; in response, others expressed their frustration at receiving pushback. "Just wondering who is the voice for these women?" one lady wrote of Jennifer and Sarah in one of the groups. "I am an adoptive mom and I feel like they need a voice!"

"When I joined this group it was because I was heartbro-
ken about what happened to these kids and wanted to know
more. What I never expected was the amount of hate that is
posted here. Not hate only toward the Hart moms, but hate
toward all white people, foster parents, adoptive parents, les-
bians," another woman wrote in a different group. "Saying
that a white person shouldn't adopt children of color, is like
saying a gay person shouldn't adopt a straight child, it's ridic-
ulous and pretty damn racist."

The groups splintered, with some focusing on the harms
of racism and posting other stories of abuse by adoptive parents, and others trying to maintain a tone of "kindness" that
resulted in more tightly controlling critical posts.

When Tammy revealed herself publicly in one of the Facebook groups, she elicited kinder discussion than Sherry, leading
to more accusations of racism. After members raised several
hundred dollars for luggage and a bus ticket for Tammy to
return to Houston, others noted that Sherry had been pillo-
ried in the same group. Afterward, the moderator—the same
one who later fell out with Tammy—posted to the group
that, after some reflection, "I have felt convicted [sic] about
some things that have taken place in this group. Things that
may have looked like I was treating Sherry and Tammy differently." She added: "I do not normally delete posts or comments but I feel it's time to stand up for Sherry the same way
we have for Tammy."

There were also elements of homophobia in some accounts of the murder-suicide. Multiple news accounts of the
crime led with "lesbian mothers" or "woke moms" in the

headline. One opinion piece in a small-town Mississippi paper went further, using the tragedy to make clear the writer's belief that same-sex couples should not raise kids at all. In the piece, titled "Far-Reaching Ramifications of Same-Sex Marriage and Adoption," Harvey Warren writes that when kids are adopted by same-sex couples, they "decline in socializing in the general public due to taunts, labels, insults, dehumanizing attacks and ostracizing by other children, in some cases, instigated by heterosexual parents. These horrible things were happening to the six Black children driven off of the cliff in California, where 'deviancy' veered off the 'course of nature.'"

Some criticisms of the Harts were much more well-informed. Nancy Polikoff, a law professor and author of *Beyond (Straight and Gay) Marriage: Valuing All Families Under the Law*, has spent much of her career looking at how family law fails LGBTQ families. In a blog post written after the crash titled, "Yes, Jennifer and Sarah Hart Played the Lesbian Card," Polikoff, a lesbian herself, writes:

> At one time, Sarah and Jennifer Hart might have been the poster couple for same-sex marriage, a white lesbian couple who adopted two black sibling groups out of foster care . . . LGBT advocacy groups would do well to remember that many of the children in foster care and available for adoption should not be there; that the state is too quick to remove children from economically disadvantaged mothers of color, *some of them lesbian and bisexual mothers*; and that the solution to the disproportionate

number of black children in the foster care system is not
more adoption by same-sex couples but more resources
to the families those children come from.

But in the larger mainstream narrative of the case, it was
as if Tammy and Sherry didn't exist at all. Many narratives
focused on Jennifer as the ringleader, and cast Sarah as potentially another victim, although the evidence for this view is
minimal. By hyper-individualizing the story—making it about
one woman with dark psychological problems—the media
largely let the state systems that failed the birth mothers off
the hook. It let listeners and readers off the hook, too—free to
enjoy the wacky and bizarre tale without thinking of how it
came to occur.

That larger media narrative would set the tone for the public
inquest itself. The inquest, which took place over two full
days in a county building, was led by an attorney named Matthew Guichard, an older gentleman with a tanned face and
white hair, who was given to long-winded explanations at
each stage of the process.

Reporters were in attendance, but none of Sarah's or Jennifer's family members, or the birth families, were present.
The entire procedure was live-streamed on YouTube, and
some family members chose to watch from home. The point
was to ascertain the official cause of the death of the family.

Guichard called a number of law enforcement officers,
as well as a search party coordinator and the doctor who

performed the autopsy, and asked each a series of questions about the investigations they'd conducted.

Allman wasn't wrong that the evidence was shocking. A theory had developed in the interim, fueled by observations made by friends of the family, that Sarah seemed to be following the lead of her wife, that Jennifer was the sole abuser and that Sarah and the children were under her control. But testimony from Deputy Jake Slates of the California Highway Patrol complicated that theory. Slates testified that, while the vehicle was in motion, en route to California from their home in Washington, Google searches on Sarah Hart's phone revealed a deadly plan forming.

> *Can 500mg of Benadryl kill a 120-pound woman?*
> *What over the counter medications can you take to overdose?*
> *How can I easily overdose on over the counter medications?*
> *Is death by drowning relatively painless?*
> *How long does it take to die from hypothermia in water while drowning in a car?*
> *What will happen while overdosing on Benadryl?*

One of Sarah's final searches was especially brutal: *No-kill shelters for dogs.*

The autopsy of the children had revealed excessive amounts of diphenhydramine, the active ingredient in Benadryl, in their systems—Markis had the equivalent of nineteen doses in his body, Abigail fourteen, and Jeremiah eight. Sarah was found to have ingested forty-two single doses of generic diphenhydramine. "That doesn't mean that they took that number," Slates clarified. "That's just the minimum number that they would have taken at that point. They could have been given more, this is just at the time of the autopsy, when we drew the blood."

Another investigator, Timothy Roloff, worked for California Highway Patrol's multidisciplinary accident investigation team, a unit that consists of a mechanic, an engineer with a physics background, and officers trained in accident reconstruction. He said there was no evidence that any of the family members had been wearing their seat belts, and that it was clear from the airbag deployment system that the Yukon had indeed accelerated off the cliff.

The evidence was conclusive, and the jury returned the unanimous verdict after an hour of deliberation. Jennifer's and Sarah's deaths were ruled suicides, and the children's deaths were ruled "death at the hands of another other than by accident."

The facts were stark: Jennifer and Sarah had been investigated for abuse in three separate states. In Minnesota, Sarah was convicted for assaulting her daughter Abigail. At the moment of crisis, when what would have been the third CPS investigation for the family was likely to commence, the women fled with the children, hatching a plan along the way. Sarah would ingest massive amounts of diphenhydramine, and give overdoses of the medication to each of the children. Jennifer, purportedly a nondrinker, would imbibe alcohol and drive her family off a rocky cliff.

When it came to deeper causes, the police's narrative of the murder-suicide would hew to Allman's initial storytelling about women who were overwhelmed with pressures. That narrative would be echoed by several other law enforcement officers who testified at the inquest. Lieutenant Shannon Barney, the Mendocino County officer who authored the press release about Hannah's remains, gave this assessment of the case: "In my opinion, based on the total circumstances, you know, it is my belief that both Jennifer and Sarah succumbed to a lot of pressure. We may never know exactly what all those pressures were. I know they got a lot of pressure from the photograph, they had some family pressures, not necessarily negative but just a lot of stuff going on in their lives, you know, to the point that they got to the point where they made this conscious decision to end their lives this way, and take the children with them."

It's quite likely, of course, that two women raising six adopted kids would feel myriad pressures. What wasn't clearly defined in these accounts is why those pressures—*not necessarily negative pressures*—would lead them to end their lives and murder their children. Not once in the inquest was the word "murder" used. In fact, the witnesses seemed to be taking great pains to be sensitive to the families—Jennifer's and Sarah's families, that is.

Nothing was said about any of the birth families, save for Tammy, whose role in submitting her DNA sample was reduced to a passive one in Barney's telling. "We worked with the Mobile, Alabama, Police Department Detective unit, and they were able to go out and contact this individual who agreed to give us a DNA sample," Barney said, which led to the positive identification of Hannah's remains.

Even the phrasing of the inquest verdicts seemed to obscure the facts of the children's deaths. "Death at the hands of another, other than by accident" is a legal term, one of four potential outcomes a California inquest can have, but it's reminiscent of the euphemism used to describe murders of civilians by police officers, which are often referred to as "officer-involved shootings." What is drugging your family and driving them off a cliff, if not murder?

One reason people showed an unusual amount of empathy for Jen and Sarah, the perpetrators of a murder-suicide, could be that they did not fit the typical profile of the people who carry out such acts. In-depth statistics on murder-suicide rates in the United States don't exist, but a six-month analysis of news reports by the Violence Policy Center revealed that during half of 2019, more than ten murder-suicides took place each week; 90 percent of the perpetrators were men; 90 percent of the incidents involved a firearm; 65 percent involved intimate partner violence; and 81 percent occurred at home. "Family annihilators," who murder multiple members of their family, are nearly always men who have exhibited a pattern of abuse against their partner and family.

The kid-gloves treatment of the women during the official proceedings of the inquest, which included multiple mentions of the family's stress, extended the mainstream narrative of the case with all its blind spots. Even those media outlets that portrayed the women darkly provided little serious discussion of the child welfare system itself, even though official decisions had a hand in the children's lives at every single step of the way.

It's possible that a major reason the Harts escaped accountability for so long, and the children were not saved, is that many people, both inside and outside the child welfare system, held a common assumption: that these six Black children must be better off with the white women who adopted them, that whatever issues they were having as a family must have been an improvement for the children over the poor conditions of their early childhood homes. "These women look normal," the Minnesota caseworker had told the caseworker in Oregon. This assumption was pushed forward by Jen herself, in the lurid descriptions she gave of the children's pasts, and in the accounts of their disturbing behavior she shared when they came to live with her and Sarah.

Despite all the evidence to the contrary, the *Thelma & Louise* version of events, in which the women were driven to the brink, literally, by the partially unnamed, not-necessarily-negative pressures of their lives, seemed to be the official version. As the record now shows, the deaths of Markis, Hannah, Abigail, Devonte, Jeremiah, and Ciera were at the hands of another, other than by accident.

15

Best Interests of the Child

After Dontay's girlfriend, Peaches, held her stillborn daughter, Ron'Niyah, in her arms, she began a slide into darkness. One day, I picked her up from her sister's, where she was staying, and she set a small plastic baggie filled with dust in my hands—the ashes of her baby girl.

As Peaches and Ye moved from her mom's place to her sister's to a friend's, she spent her time on Instagram recording long tirades against other young women on the block, ones Dontay was spending time with. She went out some nights, like most women in their twenties, and sometimes she took Ye along.

One night in November 2019, Peaches and three-year-old Ye went to the apartment of a girl she knew, who was having a party. Peaches was given a fruit punch, and she drank some. Ye was thirsty, and she gave him some, too. But a short time later, her stomach began to hurt and she felt really weird. Ye was hurting, too, and asking to see his grandma.

Peaches called her mom, Rhoda, and then she and her son caught the bus back to Southlawn, where Rhoda lived. Rhoda asked them, "Haven't y'all ate?" She and her boyfriend left Peaches and Ye at the house and went to pick up tacos for the family.

While she was out, she got another call. Ye was passed out and unresponsive. By the time Rhoda and her man got home, Peaches and Ye were being loaded into an ambulance. At the hospital, both of them flatlined for several seconds. Drug tests would reveal PCP in the bodies of both Peaches and Ye.

PCP, a hallucinogenic drug developed as an anesthetic in the 1950s, was discontinued in the '60s because it "caused patients to become agitated, delusional, and irrational," according to the U.S. Department of Justice. It can be a powder or a liquid that can be snorted, smoked, or added to a drink. Its use has declined nationally, except in certain hotspots, like Washington, D.C., and Houston, where a 2020 study by the Houston Forensic Science Center found 271 DWI cases in which the driver tested positive for PCP in 2018 alone.

While mother and son fought for their lives, Dontay was spending the weekend in the Harris County Jail, picked up for breaking into a car. The family was in crisis. As Nathaniel worked to bail out Dontay, Rhoda spent day and night at the hospital, going from the floor her daughter was on to the floor her grandson was on.

That is, until CPS entered the scene. Rhoda wasn't able to sit with Ye after that, she says, or get any information about how he was recovering. As her daughter got better, the family got the news: Ye was now in the custody of the Texas Department of Family and Protective Services.

In the days since Dontay and his siblings passed through the Harris County juvenile and CPS courts, much had changed, and much had stayed the same. Patrick Shelton retired from the bench in 2010; his successor was Glenn Devlin, the favored attorney for appointments in Shelton's court who had been appointed to search for birth fathers in the Davis children's case. By the time Devlin took the bench, the court next door was helmed by John Phillips, Shelton's old high school classmate and colleague at the DA's office.

Since Shelton's retirement, the courts' appointment practices began to receive more and more media attention. A 2018 *Texas Tribune* report found that one attorney, Oliver Sprott, had brought in $520,000 the year before by taking on nearly 400 juvenile cases and 126 family court cases in the Harris County juvenile courts. Another, Gary Polland, was appointed to 227 juvenile cases and more than 100 family court cases, on top of other work, earning about $515,000 for his court-appointed cases that year. A state-funded study pegged the maximum number of minor juvenile cases a lawyer could reasonably handle at 230. John Phillips declined to comment to the *Tribune*, but Glenn Devlin told the outlet that "each attorney is responsible for managing their cases effectively, and ethically for their clients. I have no knowledge of their caseload."

Cronyism wasn't the only issue these courts were known for. In the 2010s, the number of minors sent to juvenile detention from Harris County started to rise dramatically. In 2014, Harris County judges sent 101 children to detention; in 2017, they sent double that number. In fact, more than one in five youth in the entire state who were sentenced to detention that year came from just two courts—those helmed by John Phillips and Glenn Devlin. Nearly all of the young people sent to detention from the three Harris County courts—96 percent—were children of color (the county is 20 percent Black and 44 percent Latino).

The Harris County Public Defender's Office filed a judicial grievance against John Phillips in 2018, accusing the judge of racial bias and prejudice. The complaint, which was dismissed after Phillips was unseated later that year, notes a specific meeting, attended by assistant district attorneys assigned to Phillips's court, during which the judge "expressed his belief that the juveniles in his court cannot be rehabilitated and that 'the only thing to do was take them out of their homes and send them away.'"

The complaint also notes two other high-profile CPS cases that made local headlines. In one 2008 case in La Porte, about half an hour from Houston, Phillips removed two boys, ages one and two, from their grandparents, with whom they had lived since birth, and ordered the children into foster care. As the *Houston Chronicle* reported at the time,

Phillips told the fifty-year-old grandparents they were "too old" to care for their grandsons because "the stark reality is there's a very good chance" they would be dead by the time the children reached their twenties.

Five years later, Phillips was recused as the judge in a case involving a twelve-year-old rape victim who wanted to keep her baby. The girl was in a foster home herself, and her foster parents expressed the desire to adopt both the girl and her child. Judge Phillips told the girl, "You and the baby are not going to be together," and placed the infant with another foster family in a different county. After a public outcry resulting from several of the journalist Lisa Falkenberg's columns about the girl, dubbed "Angela" in the *Houston Chronicle*, Phillips was replaced by another judge on the case, and mother and child were reunited and adopted together.

In another 2014 column, Falkenberg reported that Phillips's Facebook page had posts "depicting undocumented immigrants as fat and lazy, disparaging Islam, linking President Obama to terrorists, and calling the president a 'domestic terrorist.'"

Despite the bad publicity, the two judges seemed untouchable, each having been reelected multiple times. But in 2018, pressures began to mount. The *Chronicle* reported that the Justice Department was probing racial disparities in sentencing and the pay-to-play practices in Harris County's juvenile courts, and that federal authorities were asking about specific judges by name. That fall, as part of a "blue wave" in an increasingly diverse Harris County, every single one of the fifty-nine Republican judges up for reelection—including

Phillips, Devlin, and the third juvenile court judge, Michael Schneider—lost their seats to Democrats. The day after the election, Devlin made national news for releasing every young person charged with a juvenile offense on his docket, "simply asking the kids whether they planned to kill anyone before letting them go," the *Chronicle* reported. "Apparently he was saying that's what the voters wanted," one public defender told the paper.

By the time Ye's case reached the 315th District Court, the presiding judge was Leah Shapiro, a former public defender. In addition to the normal caseload of CPS and juvenile cases, Shapiro and her associate judge, Dena Fisher, run a special "dual status" docket, focused on youth who are involved in both the child welfare and juvenile justice systems. Tara Grigg Green, of the Foster Care Advocacy Center, said that since the judges have turned over, the appointment system has seemed more fair. She did note, however, that on hundreds of old cases, which often take years to cycle through, the attorneys appointed by the former judges remain at work, becoming grandfathered in.

The rampant cronyism seems to have died down in the Harris County juvenile courts, and with the change in judges has come a return to obscurity. No recent high-profile stories of judges bungling child welfare cases have hit the local papers. Still, untold numbers of children and families passed through these courts in the decades between Shelton's election in 1994 up through 2019, when his buddies finally gave up their seats. And those children have become adults, who often have children of their own. Research has shown that having a parent with experience in the foster care system increases the likelihood that a child enters the system. Ye is just one of the many children whose involvement with the child welfare system is intergenerational.

And here in the juvenile court complex in downtown Houston, the courts still churn through the cases. The county attorneys still file a motion for termination of parental rights immediately upon removing a child, as is the standard practice in Texas, so if the parents slip up, the paperwork for termination is ready to go. CPS's mandatory service plans, in theory meant to help struggling parents, are often unwieldy and require working with social services on problems the parents aren't known to have, giving already overwhelmed moms and dads a laundry list of tasks without providing much if any support for them. Even just one incomplete piece of the service plan constitutes grounds for termination of the parents' rights. Things are much quieter in the juvenile courts these days, but in many ways, it is still business as usual.

After the Hart family crash, I reached out to Pat Shelton, who by 2018 was retired from his legal practice. Over about thirty minutes, we spoke about the children's case and about some of the contentious allegations of his courtroom conduct that journalists reported locally while he was on the bench. He called the allegations of pay-to-play appointments "totally inaccurate."

He said he didn't remember Davis's children specifically. "We had hundreds of adoptions done in every court that deals with these cases," he told me. But it was clear he was following the case; he knew details of the Harts' alleged abuse and their deaths.

Shelton spoke in a general way about their case. He said that he was sure CPS had tried to place the children locally, and then in-state, before pursuing out-of-state adoption. "There are a number of children that are posted on a nationwide network. Particularly if there are groups of children, that's sometimes what it takes," Shelton said, adding that "Minnesota has been very helpful overall in providing folks who have an interest in adoptions."

I asked him how the Harts were allowed to adopt Devonte, Jeremiah, and Ciera after an allegation of abuse had already been made against the women. Shelton said that the lack of criminal charges in that case would most likely have made it pass under the radar of officials in Texas. "Unless there's a criminal charge, what can you do?" Shelton said. "Believe it or not, kids get bruises that do not get beat."

Shelton sounded tired. There were moments when his breathing was so heavy over the phone, I thought he might be in distress. He brought up local Houston journalists who had written about him decades before by name, and railed against their reporting, saying that because he was a judge, he was never allowed to publicly defend himself. He denied that he, or his associate judge Robert Molder, favored nonrelative adoptions over placements with family members. "We have been disappointed by so many relatives before, that act like kids are the property of the parents, and they'll say what they need to say just to get the kids back to the parent . . . and it's not just the parent, it's whoever else in their life, typically a crummy boyfriend, especially when drugs are on the scene," Shelton told me, his voice agitated, before we got off the phone. "You're trying to say, wait a second, you've got to have perfect crystal-ball knowledge of how somebody's gonna fare in Minnesota and second-guess yourself on everything you did."

It wasn't until a week before Christmas, more than a month after CPS took custody of Ye, that Dena Fisher, the associate judge in the 315th District Court, held a placement hearing for him. The first two court hearings were reset, because the hospital hadn't sent the medical records—about a thousand pages of them—to the attorneys until just before the hearing. Peaches and the rest of the family had dressed to the nines for these hearings, waiting patiently in the courtroom only to have the judge abruptly reset the dates. Then the families sat in a pretrial mediation hearing, which is private and not open to reporters, but no consensus was reached on where to place the three-year-old. By the time the first placement hearing actually took place, Ye was out of the hospital, having recovered, and was staying in a foster home. At the court that day, it looked like the separation from Ye was getting to Peaches. Gone were the fancy outfits; she was dressed in leggings and a shirt, with her hair pulled back, and her face, free of makeup, was serious and scared. Dontay did not show up.

Since she regained consciousness in the hospital, Peaches had tried to explain to her lawyer, and to the caseworker, that she didn't know what was in that drink. She thought it was a misunderstanding, something she could clear up once she got the chance to speak to a judge. But in these court hearings, parents don't get the chance to speak; their attorneys speak on their behalf, and the judge, who sees dozens of cases each week, didn't seem to have much time for the parents' attorneys' objections, either.

Peaches and her mother had been able to see Ye in two supervised visits in the month since he was removed from her care. In both visits, she said, Ye showed up in the same outfit, and although he had been potty trained, she noticed he was back in Pampers. His hair wasn't done, and there were rashy bumps on his face. She was worried about him, and she wanted her son to come home.

Both Rhoda and Nathaniel had asked to get temporary custody while their children worked their case plans, which included drug testing, parenting classes, and psychological evaluations. But CPS was concerned that Nathaniel, in his late seventies, was too old, and when they went to do a home study on Rhoda's place, they smelled marijuana smoke in the apartment complex. The county attorney also noted that during the PCP incident Ye had been taken by ambulance from Rhoda's home, which seemed to imply that Ye might have ingested the drugs at his grandmother's house.

The judge ordered that Ye stay put in his foster home that day, dashing the family's hopes of having him home by Christmas. Peaches's attorney, Ryan Mitchell, asked the judge if his client could see her child on Christmas Day. The judge asked the caseworker, who said she'd have to ask Ye's foster parents. If not Christmas Day, the judge told her, find out when they can visit.

Once she left the courtroom, Peaches broke down. "I act like nothing's wrong, I act strong, but inside I'm broken. I lost my baby girl and now I can't barely see my baby boy," she said through tears, slumped on a bench in the hallway of the court, amid the bustle of worried parents and scared teens, some of them in orange jumpsuits and shackles, waiting their turn in juvenile court. Peaches was so upset, she wasn't able to hold back her tears; she wept openly. "He's my everything. I see people with their kids and their babies and I ain't got mine."

Outside the courthouse, an old Black man in a Santa hat played his trumpet, with the instrument case open at his feet for tips. The day was cold, and the downtown office workers shuffled quickly from one place to the next. The solitary horn, playing "O Little Town of Bethlehem," carried in the air for a block in each direction.

By February 2020, the family was feeling optimistic that Ye would be able to stay with Nathaniel while Peaches and Dontay continued to work their case plans. He'd been through the home study, and given caseworkers the names of his nieces and daughter, who would help him with Ye if he needed it. Nathaniel still had a clean record, and didn't have any vices at all, besides his Coca-Cola, which he calls "soda water."

He was slowing down due to his age, that was true. His knee hurt all the time, and he took pain medication to manage it. But he knew he could hold it together for his family, because they needed him, and Ye needed to be home.

They even cleared Dontay's room in Nathaniel's home, making Ye his own space: A big multicolored rug was spread out over the carpet, with a blue toddler bed up against the window. New toys, purchased for his arrival, were stacked on a bookshelf. A brand-new Super Soaker—Peaches just knew Ye would love it—was laid proudly on the windowsill.

But in March, the Covid-19 pandemic hit, and the entire court system, and every other facet of life, was upended. Gone were in-person court hearings; the judges went to a bare-bones rotation system and held only show-cause hearings, in which CPS makes its case for taking temporary custody of a child, for several weeks. The judges turned their attention to the juvenile docket, trying to resolve low-level cases to get as many children as possible out of detention, where they had an increased risk of contracting Covid-19.

The courts, already proceeding at a glacial pace, were further slowed down, and the Adoption and Safe Families Act's rules for closing cases expeditiously were suspended due to the pandemic. Ye did not return to Nathaniel; his cheerfully decorated room sat empty. On March 30, Ye turned four. Peaches wanted to bring him cupcakes, but the caseworker told her in-person visits were suspended. Instead, she Face-Timed him on his birthday. "I feel lost about my baby," she told me. "I'm worried because he could get sick; he gets sick easily." She texted her caseworker regularly to ask about him.

"In the midst of all this going on," she said, "he'd normally be with me."

As the case unfolded, Ye's family often did not have a clear understanding of what was happening, either in the courtroom or outside it. After private mediation sessions the family would often call me in a panic; I'd call their attorneys and get a sense of what was happening, and then I'd call the family back and explain it in a way they could understand. The rapid pace of the court, especially as it proceeded via Zoom hearings due to Covid-19, was unforgiving and seemed at odds with the time it would take to explain things to the family clearly.

In court hearings, the state's argument never really changed, and it never sounded good for the family. Gloria Glover, the county attorney, argued that Ye should stay in a foster home and that there were no adequate family placements for him. Glover said neither parent was compliant with their service plans, having missed appointments and skipped classes.

Peaches was clearly trying, her attorney argued; her parenting classes were under way, and the biggest hurdle in the completion of her service plan was the fact that all services went virtual during the pandemic, and Peaches did not have steady access to Wi-Fi. In fact, in Zoom court hearings, she often cut out for minutes at a time, her connection dropping and coming back on at random. At one point, a continuance was granted, pushing the trial date back several months, because Peaches could not stay connected to the Wi-Fi long enough to understand what the judge was saying. After that, her lawyer had to get special permission for Peaches to attend court in person.

Although Peaches was struggling, she was clearly making an effort. She never missed a visit with her son once the in-person visitation was reinstated, and she brought him clothes and gifts and McDonald's for lunch, snapping photos of them hugging and dancing in the CPS offices.

Dontay, on the other hand, wasn't as consistent, and the chances he would retain rights to Ye were slim from the beginning. Ye's caseworker testified that Dontay tested positive for drugs several times, usually for marijuana, and didn't show up to multiple scheduled visits with his son. Glover, the county attorney, told the judge that Dontay was combative and that he wouldn't even give them his current address. Dontay, of course, was in the midst of his worst nightmare—he was grown, and he was out of foster care, but through his son, he was right back there dealing with the people he hated most.

The case crept along, and Ye had another birthday, his fifth. Finally, the opening of the trial was set for May 2021. Just days ahead of that, the family again sat in mediation. Rhoda was present at the session, and later described an anguished Dontay explaining to the room what happened to him in foster care, and what happened to his siblings. "I don't want what happened to me to happen to him," Dontay said about his son. According to Rhoda, the caseworker replied, "That was then, this is now."

After mediation, Peaches's attorney, Ryan Mitchell, and Thao Tran, who represented Dontay, gave the parents advice that terrified the entire family. During the course of Ye's case, Peaches had become pregnant by Dontay again; she was due to give birth in June. But because she was required to take drug tests regularly as part of Ye's case, and she tested positive for cocaine in March, her attorney told her that her rights to her new baby were at risk.

Because of a controversial statute in the Texas Family Code, under certain circumstances CPS is legally able to take newborn babies from their mothers if they have previously and involuntarily lost their parental rights to another child. If a court found that a child was "knowingly placed . . . in conditions or surroundings which endanger the physical or emotional well-being of the child," or if a mother were to test positive for drugs or otherwise be accused of harming her child at birth, a mother's subsequent children could be removed at the hospital, and CPS would not even need to provide services to the mother before terminating her rights to her new baby. (This statute, which advocates claimed violated the rights of mothers, was struck from the Texas Family Code as part of a 2021 overhaul of the definitions of abuse and neglect. Peaches, however, had no way to foresee the change in the law.)

Peaches was hysterical; she already felt like she was approaching her breaking point, and if she lost her new baby, she would be destroyed. Her attorney stressed that this statute would apply only if CPS had reasonable grounds to take the baby; still, the failed drug test didn't look good for Peaches, he said, and he was concerned that she might not be clean when she was tested again at the time of the birth.

He told her she could avoid this nightmare scenario if

she relinquished her rights to Ye voluntarily. By doing so, she would avoid a termination under these serious circumstances, referred to as D and E grounds for the way they are listed in the family code. Dontay's lawyer gave him the same advice. But neither parent wanted to give their rights to Ye away; they wanted him to know that they fought for him, that they wanted him. They told their attorneys they would take the case to trial.

The first day of the trial, all of the parties joined Zoom. Peaches and her lawyer were in separate attorney briefing rooms on the same floor of the courthouse, logged in to laptops. Dontay was represented by his own attorney, but he was not there; I had gone to Nathaniel's apartment earlier that day to pick up Nathaniel and Dontay, but Dontay refused to come. "My stomach hurts," he told me on the phone as I sat in the parking lot outside his house. Nathaniel, looking frail and wearing a knit cap pulled over his ears, came out to the car. "He won't do it," he told me.

Nathaniel told me they would not let him call in to the hearing, since, as a grandparent, he wasn't technically a party to the case, and he was terrified of catching Covid at the courthouse, since he was an old man with a lengthy list of health problems. "I ain't gon' let them kill me," he told me, and I could see the fear in his eyes. He chose to stay home, and I told him I would call him afterward and let him know Ye's fate.

As a journalist, I also was not a party to the case, but

since the proceedings were public, I was allowed to attend by going into the courthouse. In the courtroom, I was completely alone; a large TV was set up, and I could watch the Zoom proceedings from there. It was eerie; the usually bustling floor where the juvenile and CPS courts were located was almost completely empty, save for a bailiff and a court administrator. Judge Dena Fisher was logged in from her home, as were the rest of the parties present, including the court-appointed special advocate and Ye's attorney, Dani Rosenblum.

Gloria Glover, the county attorney, was also logged in from home. On her lap bounced her own baby, seemingly home from day care due to the pandemic. This wasn't the first of Ye's hearings Glover attended while rocking her baby; no one brought it up in court, but outside court, Rhoda, Peaches's mom, expressed her displeasure that the attorney could sit in court holding her own baby while arguing to take Rhoda's daughter's baby away from her.

Both Dontay's and Peaches's attorneys requested another continuance, which would delay the trial another couple of months, but Judge Fisher had no patience this time around for their arguments about the difficulty of completing services during the Covid pandemic. Trial was to begin, she ruled, and Gloria Glover called her first witness, Ye's caseworker, Gabrielle Bernal.

"The child is currently in an adoptive home. Is that right?" Glover asked.

"That is correct," Bernal replied.

"Okay. And how long has he been there?"

"Since November 2020."

"How old is [Ye]?"

"He is five years old," Bernal said.

"Have you ever had any conversations with [Ye] regarding what he wants?"

"He would like to stay in his current home," Bernal replied.

At this, Peaches, on mute, looked as if she cried out in pain. Tears started streaming down her face, and she shook her head. *No, no, no.*

"Does it appear that [Ye] is bonded with this placement?" Glover went on, rocking her baby.

"Yes, yes."

"And why would you say that?"

"In our car rides together, he will talk about the foster parent and the home environment and the people he gets to see, that they have together. And he just appears like he's gotten attached, and has started referring to the foster parents as parents," Bernal responded.

Things were clearly not looking good for Peaches and Dontay at the trial. The county attorney and Ye's caseworker noted that there was currently a warrant out for Dontay's arrest for committing domestic violence against Peaches. A restraining order had been filed, Glover said, but the caseworker testified that on a visit to Peaches's home, she saw Dontay at the apartment complex.

After Glover finished with her questions, Tran, Dontay's attorney, got a chance to cross-examine the caseworker.

"I know you testified earlier that the father did engage in

parenting class and some drug testing. Is that correct?" Tran asked Bernal.

"Yes."

"And did the father explain to you repeatedly that he did not have transportation?"

"Yes, he did say that."

"Did the agency do anything to assist in transporting the father to do the services?"

"No, we did not."

"Now, you understand that the father, he is a foster child himself. Is that correct?"

"Yes."

"And would you agree that he's expressed his trauma as a foster child? Correct?"

"Yes."

It was the first time, a year and a half after Ye was removed from his mom and placed in foster care, that it came up in court that Dontay was himself a foster youth. Still, no one mentioned that day that his three siblings had also been in care, that Dontay had been separated from them without warning, and that they had been killed in the care of their adoptive parents three years prior.

As Tran finished her questioning, the trial had been under way for a little less than an hour. During normal times, in-person court hearings often run long, with 9:00 a.m. hearings sometimes delayed until the afternoon, with parties waiting nervously as the judge slowly works through the docket. But in Covid times, Zoom court hearings were precise, and Judge Fisher had an adversary hearing scheduled for 3:00 p.m.

Abruptly, the trial was paused, and a new court date was set to finish it up. Because of the backlog of cases, there wasn't an open date until July 20, nearly three months later. The family was bewildered. They'd expected a decision that day, and they were prepared for the worst; nobody expected the trial to just not finish. From the tenor so far, it seemed unlikely Peaches and Dontay would keep their rights to their son. The family wasn't sure if the pause simply delayed the crushing blow they were bracing for, but they breathed a sigh of relief anyway; they'd happily take visits with Ye for a couple more months. Peaches was due June 21; Ye might even get a chance to meet his baby brother.

Right on time, Peaches's new baby was born. She showed him off in the hospital on an Instagram livestream. Where Ye favored his grandma Sherry and looked a lot like his uncle Devonte, the new baby was the spitting image of Peaches, with light skin and big round eyes. She took to calling him Legs, because his skinny little legs were so long compared to his tiny body. He began to nurse immediately with no problems, and the two of them stayed in the hospital for several days. Peaches's drug test was clean, and she was able to briefly go home with the baby. But soon, CPS came to her with an offer.

Because she was currently involved in a CPS case, her caseworker asked her to voluntarily place Legs with an approved family member, as part of a safety plan. What the department calls a safety plan, several legal experts call "hidden foster care," the practice of asking parents to voluntarily send their children to family members without opening a court case. Because there is no case, there is no way to track the number of "soft removals," but the legal scholar Josh Gupta-Kagan guesses that these types of removals may be as frequent as traditional removals—potentially doubling the size of the system's influence on families. In 2014, Texas used soft removals thirty-four thousand times, according to a state-issued report on the issue. These safety plans are often used in cases of substance use, but Gupta-Kagan and others are concerned about how voluntary these removals actually are. "It is as if a police department investigated a crime, concluded an individual was guilty, did not file charges or provide him with an attorney, and told him he had to agree to go to jail for several weeks or months, or else it would bring him to court and things could get even worse," Gupta-Kagan wrote in a *Stanford Law Review* article about the practice.

A soft removal is often offered as an alternative to having a case with CPS initiated. Because a CPS case increases the likelihood of the child ending up with a stranger, Gupta-Kagan and other legal advocates say it's inherently coercive. Moreover, lawyers don't get appointed in CPS cases until a case is initiated, most often after a child is removed, so advocates worry that these safety plans are often instituted in cases in which the agency might not have sufficient evidence to remove a child if it took the matter to court. It's likely parents don't know what their rights would be in such a situation. In 2020, a federal appeals court ruled that a Kentucky couple could sue social workers who allegedly threatened to remove their children if the parents didn't agree to a "prevention plan" after the mother claimed she received a false-positive drug test.

In a court, CPS needs "to show abuse or neglect, that the child is in significant imminent risk of harm from that abuse or neglect, and show that the removal is necessary to protect the child," Gupta-Kagan said. "The question you have to ask is, How much do you really trust CPS agencies to get all of that right all of the time, such that they should be allowed to do this without any due process checks?"

For Peaches, though, who had spent her last months of pregnancy terrified that CPS would remove her new baby at birth, the safety plan seemed like a good choice. Her relationship with her father was strained, and she knew that her mother wouldn't be able to take the baby, as her home study had not been approved. She called her paternal aunt, Dorothy Watkins, who worked in the billing department of a local children's hospital. Dorothy agreed to take in the baby, and she and Peaches signed an agreement saying that Peaches would have only supervised visits with the new baby.

"I'm relieved," Peaches told me by phone. "I really think it's what I need."

There was another advantage to doing things this way. Because Dorothy was an accepted placement for the baby, she would likely be given genuine consideration to take in Ye as well. She notified the court that she would like Ye to be placed with her. There were several trial dates in the ensuing months, but because attorneys and caseworkers seemed to only open the case file the week of the trial date—likely because they were overloaded with cases—none of the needed paperwork was ready by the time court was in session. The July date turned into an October date, which then turned into a date just before Christmas. An hourlong portion of the trial took place in April 2022, during which Mitchell, Peaches's attorney, took part in heated questioning of the caseworker. After months of delays, during which CPS dragged its feet on completing a home study of Dorothy Watkins—including waiting four months to sign the completed home study once a caseworker had recommended that it be approved—the department had finally signed off on Dorothy as a suitable placement. This was the news the Davis family had been waiting for: Neither Rhoda nor Nathaniel had passed the home study required to take Ye in, but now, Dorothy had—and since she was also caring for Ye's baby brother, she seemed likely to get Ye, too, which would return the boy to his extended family.

But CPS made clear in court that day that despite an approved home study, the agency did not want Ye to be placed with his aunt. The caseworker testified that his "needs are very different than his brother's; [he] has PTSD. He has experienced immense trauma and he's very well established at his current foster home and moving him would be traumatic."

"You testified earlier that one of the reasons why you're not removing [Ye] from the foster placement is because of bonding with the caregiver. Correct?" Mitchell asked the caseworker on cross-examination, who responded, "Yes."

"So for the first three years of his life, for half of that kid's life, he was placed with his mother, correct?" he asked.

"Yes."

"And then for four months, there was a delay in potentially placing him with Ms. Watkins because DFPS had to get a signature, correct?"

"Yes."

"Okay. And then that program director signed off on that approved home study in October of 2021. Correct?"

"Yes."

"But for the last six months, DFPS has refused to place him with Watkins even though there is an approved home study with his family and with his brother?"

"Yes."

Mitchell's point was made: DFPS had tacked on an additional 10 months of time to Ye's placement with a foster parent, during which the caregiver declared a wish to adopt, and the bonding they'd held up as a reason to keep him there was heavily influenced by CPS's delays.

After an hour, the trial was again cut short, but the parties still needed more time to make their case. Ye entered care in November 2019; he'd had three birthdays since then. The trial to determine whether or not Peaches and Dontay would have their parental rights terminated began in July 2021. A year later, the trial would still not be finished. As the months and years went by, and as Ye continued to grow, Peaches and Dontay continued to wait, unsure whether he would come back to their family or if they'd be legally severed from their son forever.

16

A Final Resting Place

Since the day I first set foot in Sherry's apartment, two weeks after her children had been driven off a cliff, I had known of the family's desire to bring them home. Watching Tammy beg the Mendocino County Sheriff's Office to connect her with Jennifer's and Sarah's parents, to no avail, I realized I might be in a unique position to help. I told her I would try to reach them, and make it known that the birth families wanted their children's remains home with them.

I hadn't planned on reaching out to Jennifer's or Sarah's family members at all. They'd been hounded by the media, first when the crash happened and then again when the inquest took place in April, a year after their daughters' deaths. Alan and Brenda Gengler turned down all media requests, and so did Sarah's two brothers. Brenda had been quoted just once, in a story in *Sonoma Magazine*, when she told the reporter that hearing about what happened to Sarah was like hearing about a ghost. "Most of us have been grieving for the last 17 years," she said. "She chose Jen over us, for life."

Doug Hart, Jennifer's father, had spoken to *The Oregonian* for a story about Jen's life, so I thought I would begin with him. In November 2019, I found several email addresses that might be his and sent a note to all of them. I sent him the stories I had written about the families, and told him they had a deep desire to have the ashes back, or to at least know if and where the children had been buried.

Several hours later, he responded, and we began to talk on the phone. "First of all," he said right away, "considering the circumstances, I believe that the natural-born parents deserve the right to know, and more so I feel it would be proper that they do have the cremains."

After the story about Jennifer's life came out in *The Oregonian*, Doug was really upset. The reporter was the one person he had chosen to speak to; she was from the area, and she had sat with him in his house for several hours as he "tried to put a positive spin on things," he says. "I poured my heart out to her," he added, "and she stabbed me in the back."

The piece in *The Oregonian* wasn't a hit job, by any means, but the facts of the family's story were what they were, and they were not good for Jen. "It talked about the adopting parents and how evil they were," he said. At the time the article had run, Doug had doubted the deaths were intentional; he'd asked his friends and family why two women would go to all this trouble to raise these children, and then kill them. "Why would you go through everything you did and end it this way?"

He softened toward the reporter a bit after the inquest,

when he realized the version of events he'd hoped and prayed was true was not what actually happened. "I wanted in my heart, I wanted to believe it was an accident, it was not an intentional act," he said. "Obviously, they proved me wrong. Why they chose to do that, I don't know. It's beyond my comprehension."

And while he believed now that the birth parents should be able to have the remains of their children, the problem was that he didn't have them, and he wasn't exactly sure where they were.

Following the crash, and after the autopsies, the bodies of the family—besides those of Hannah and Devonte, who were still missing—were cremated and given to Sarah's father, Alan Gengler. Alan, with one of his sons, had driven his truck out to Washington to clear out the Hart family home. He'd then driven down to California to retrieve the remains.

On the way back, he stopped to speak with Doug. The two had never met or even spoken to each other. The Genglers had, in their minds, lost their daughter to Jennifer, whom they saw as manipulative, and now, after years of not speaking, they'd learned the worst possible thing had happened. Doug, for his part, wanted the women to be buried together, as married partners.

Alan directed Doug to a storage area where he could retrieve ten or so big plastic tubs of items from the Hart home that the Genglers had deemed were Jennifer's personal effects. When he picked up the tubs, Doug said, the rest of the home's items—furniture, the family's other car—were nowhere in sight. Alan gave him his daughter's ashes, too.

So Jennifer's ashes were in his garage, Doug said, along with the ashes of her beloved childhood cat. The tubs, full of thousands of photos Jennifer had taken of her life, from childhood through college and including many of the kids, were also nestled in the garage.

After the crash, Jen's family had initially planned a celebration of her life, which would be a service for those close to her pending a formal burial, but it had been canceled. Doug said he scanned hundreds of Jen's photographs for a slideshow for the event, and when they couldn't figure out how to make the technology for the slideshow work, he didn't want to go through with it. But it was also true that as days and weeks went by, more and more troubling information was coming out about the family's history with Child Protective Services, and that made holding the event seem undesirable. Tensions between Doug and his ex-wife, Deb, weren't helping the plans get straightened out, either.

According to Doug, Deb and her son Christopher said that Jen had once told them that she didn't want to be buried in South Dakota. Rather, she wanted her ashes to be spread across the mountains of the Pacific Northwest. Doug bristled at this idea; he thought the family should be buried in South Dakota, where the women were from. Deb and Doug had never been able to get along since their divorce. And the communication between the Harts and the Genglers, already strained, began to break down as well. Doug hadn't spoken to Alan in months, he said, and he wasn't sure if the children had been buried or not.

"The longer this goes on, the harder it's going to be," he said. "They need a final resting place."

I thought it was unlikely the Genglers would ever cooperate in releasing the children's remains. But I hoped that Doug might share the pictures, artwork, and other artifacts in his garage with the birth families, and that this might mean a lot to them.

Exactly a year after we first spoke, in October 2020, Doug called me with an explicit request. He said he felt legally entitled to 25 percent of the children's remains, seeing as the legal proceedings involving the family's estate had split the estate four ways among each of the Hart and Gengler parents. He asked me if I would reach out to Alan for him—communication had ended completely by then—and request that Alan release that portion of the remains to me, on Doug's behalf.

I was overwhelmed by the request. I had been reporting on this story for more than two years at this point, and had developed relationships with the birth families that were much deeper than those I make in the regular course of my journalism work. I'd learned about the families' histories, traumas, and fears, and I felt it was only right for them to have some of their children's remains. The families wanted badly for this to happen, and I knew deep down that it was unlikely a better chance would arise to make it so.

Doug had been alternately hot and cold with me when I'd reached out throughout the year, possibly not sure that he could trust a reporter at all. In my one conversation with Alan, he declined to be interviewed; I knew that he wouldn't love hearing from me again. But, I figured, I had to try. I sent Alan an email matter-of-factly detailing Doug's request, and saying that I planned to come to South Dakota in a week. Time was of the essence, because winter was coming, and the long drive I'd be making from Houston would get increasingly difficult once snow was on the ground.

When I spoke with Alan on the phone, he seemed to be on speaker, since I could hear his wife, Brenda, clearly. She said the birth families didn't deserve anything, in her opinion, and that she had documents from the children's cases that detailed why. I told her I would love to see those documents, as many records are sealed, and could go through them with the couple when I was in South Dakota the following week.

Alan sounded tired of fighting, and he said he figured Doug had a legal right to those remains. He agreed to relinquish the asked-for 25 percent, as long as I enlisted a professional to do the dividing, and that it came at no cost to him. I agreed, reaching out to a local funeral home in the Genglers' hometown, whose owners agreed to take part in this rather strange request, with no fee for their services.

All of a sudden, after a year of no progress, the time was finally here to tell the birth families that they could get their wish.

A week later, I was on the road driving straight north from Houston, Texas, through the heartland toward the frigid border of South Dakota and Minnesota. I never saw Alan or Brenda. I went straight to the funeral home, where Alan had dropped the ashes, and sat with the friendly folks there as they respectfully divided the remains, taking care to make sure they got it right. The Genglers kept a portion of the children's remains, presumably to bury them in South Dakota. The ashes of the children were put in ziplock bags, and divided by birth family into lush red velvet pouches. The pouch for Tammy included the remains of Markis and Abigail's bodies, and a tiny packet of the partial remains found of Hannah. The Davis family would get the remains of Jeremiah and Ciera, but not Devonte, who has never been found.

After the remains were divided, I called Alan to let him know it was done, and asked if we could meet. He told me that he and his wife wouldn't be speaking with me any further, and that they would not be willing to share the documents in their possession.

I was disappointed. In our last planning conversation, just he and I, we worked out how we'd make the transfer, and he requested that I get the birth mothers to confirm their desire for the remains through emails directly to him. It had felt that his stance was softening; he sounded more tired than angry, and I was hoping he might be ready to share more about his family.

I wouldn't understand until I drove down to Huron the next day that there had been a big argument between Alan and Doug in the interim, in the week between when we made the plan and when I executed it. Doug had lost his temper on a call, threatening legal action after he sensed Alan planned to move forward with the burial of Sarah's remains and the remainder of the children's remains—without Jennifer's. "I said I don't care what you think about my daughter and me and the rest of my family, I said Jennifer and Sarah were married and this is the way they would want it. Jennifer and Sarah and the kids need to be buried together," Doug told me as we spoke, masked and distanced, in his garage.

The detached garage was very clean, with a black Porsche inside and an electric fireplace heater that made the space warm while the weather hovered in the teens outside. After Doug opened up a plastic table so I could go through the tubs and tubs of Jennifer's things stacked against the wall, he left me there for hours while he puttered around inside on phone calls.

It was strange and upsetting looking through the items Jennifer had chosen to save from her life. A birthday card from her grandma for her sixth birthday. Letters full of crude humor her uncle had written to her mother from prison, where he was serving his life sentence for murder. Cheesy art from high school and college; a large and rudimentary self-portrait in a red jacket, and another, with shorter hair and an eyebrow piercing. She wasn't a talented artist. There was an entire tub full of Barack Obama memorabilia, including a commemorative plate and a bobblehead doll.

And, of course, there were a lot of things in the tubs that related to the children. Jennifer had saved some of their clothes in plastic bags, including the matching "Thing 1, Thing 2" shirts they were seen wearing in photos on Facebook. There was a small, light pink dress with a polo collar,

striped with white and green, that Ciera had worn the day
she'd met Jennifer and Sarah. A handwritten note was tucked
into the bag, clearly in hopes that Ciera would one day come
to possess the dress:

> This is the dress you were wearing the day we first met
> you. Your hair was done up in many tiny braids & beads.
> You smiled so big when we held you for the first time . . .
> so sweet. You instantly trusted us, and we instantly fell
> in love! A day I will always cherish and remember. Love,
> Moms

There were other notes, to other children, each with an
accompanying shirt or artifact: Deflated balloons from the
day Devonte, Jeremiah, and Ciera came to live with them.
Shirts from Obama's inauguration; "You said you were trad-
ing in this shirt and wearing your suit!" she wrote to Devonte.
These notes were clearly written at a time when Jennifer envisioned the children, grown up, taking these little keepsakes
along with them.

There was also a postcard from the Permanent Family
Resource Center with a color photo of Hannah kissing Sarah
on the cheek. On the photo in white Comic Sans font were
the words "Celebrate Adoption, Consider Adoption . . . Children are Waiting!"

By the time Doug came in and sat down to talk, it had
been several hours. My head was filled with a lot of feelings that confused me. It would feel very intimate to look
through any stranger's things, the artifacts she chose to save

for herself from her lifetime. It was darker to do so when
the person in question murdered six children. Unlike many
who'd investigated the Harts' story, I was not drawn in by
Jennifer's and Sarah's psychological motivations. What mo-
tivated me most was to see, and to share, the parts of the
story that had been made invisible: The real and complicated
families these children came from. The children themselves.
And the involvement of a system that directed the course of
their short lives, a system that remained unaccountable for
their deaths.

But here I was, sitting in a warm, empty garage, reading
notes from Jennifer's high school friends and looking at her
amateur art. I understood why Doug had told me the year
before, when we first spoke, that he hadn't been emotionally
prepared to go through the tubs yet. I also got a sense that
that was why he'd asked me here: he wanted the birth families to have some of these precious things, but he didn't want
to look at them himself.

Doug was a big man with white hair cut in a flattop
army style. In a state that was about to be hit harder by
Covid than any other, with residents telling hospital nurses
that they didn't believe in the virus even as they were dying
from it, Doug was taking the pandemic very seriously. He
had chronic obstructive pulmonary disorder from a bad lung
infection, and since he was retired, he was spending most of
his time alone, or getting things ready up north in Minnesota, where he'd bought a vacation home. He was a Huron
native, and a heartland man, with a voice like John Good-
man's, and on the below-freezing day that we met, he was

wearing a hooded sweatshirt, basketball shorts, and slip-on shoes.

I had told Doug that I wanted to hear about Jennifer's childhood, and he said he hesitated to share. Many reporters had reached out; he'd felt hounded. Avoiding the media was the main reason he'd chosen to skip the inquest, choosing instead to watch it online. "Why should I go on TV or the radio or any kind of media and share my side of the story, thinking I'm going to sway some boats my way? Ain't gonna change a thing."

Still, he wanted to talk about what he saw as flaws in the child welfare system. In his mind, it started back when the two states agreed to give the women more children than anyone could reasonably handle. "When I learned of the first three, I could say, 'Well, I'm happy for them, because here's three children that will have a chance in life.' But when I was informed that they adopted three more, all I could do was sit there and do this," he said, shaking his head. "I'm going, *What in the world are they thinking? What in the world is the adoption services thinking to allow this to happen?*"

He continued, "Sometimes—it's my opinion, and just my opinion—I think that people might do it for the money. I'm not pointing any fingers. I don't know if Jennifer and Sarah got a stipend or not—"

They did, I told him.

"Did they?"

Yes, Texas does provide that, I said.

"So at the end of the day, did they do it for the kids or the stipend? I want to believe otherwise, but I know the

world we live in. Either way, six children is too many. No
state should ever allow anyone to adopt that many children.
Period."

I said that there were signs of abuse before the second set
of kids were legally adopted; if being overwhelmed was the
issue, why would they choose to continue? It was clear that
he had read and taken in the detailed accounts of abuse, but
that he was having trouble squaring those facts with the way
he saw his daughter in his mind.

"I don't know what went on behind the scenes. You
know, all I know is what I've read. To me it's hearsay. Everybody has their way of parenting. Did they withhold food
to punish them? I don't know, I wasn't there. I know my
daughter—I want to believe my daughter has my heart, and
I know I would never do that. I couldn't do that. If I felt the
need to punish my child or my pet, it wouldn't be by *withholding food*," he says, looking bewildered. "I want to believe that
even though we were apart, she still had a good part of me in
her and she would never do anything . . . But, once again, I
wasn't there, so I don't know if that happened."

On the way out, he asked me not to visit with Deb or his
son Christopher, who also lived in Huron. They didn't know
what he was doing with the remains, or with his daughter's
things. "I personally feel the birth parents are entitled to
something. I'm doing this because I want them to have some
sort of closure, and if this will help that, then that's what I
want to do."

As we ended our conversation, I grabbed the things I
had set aside for the birth families. I took Ciera's pink dress

with the green stripes, which I thought Sherry might like. (I pulled the note out of the bag; I knew she wouldn't want that.) I found a thick folder of Devonte's colored-pencil drawings, many with spiritual themes, Native American imagery, and lots and lots of interesting-looking people of all shades; some of the drawings looked inspired by the Beloved Festivals they used to attend. And I went through each and every one of the thousands of photographs, pulling the ones that had only the children in them, and dividing them into two piles; those for Tammy, and those for the Davises. Still, all the items fit in one small cardboard box.

"Is that all you've got?" Doug asked me, disappointedly.

I told him I knew the families wanted photos, but that much of the stuff Jennifer saved was of a family life that the birth families were not a part of.

"I'm kind of sad that you're not taking more stuff for them," he told me as he walked me out to my car. "That's your call. At least they have the cremains, and they have some mementos, and that's more than they had before you started this journey."

It was past Christmas when I was finally able to return the remains to the birth families. Sherry, who holds her grief tightly to her chest, asked that I leave the ashes with Nathaniel.

When I met him on the front steps of his apartment, Nathaniel looked especially worn and tired. We sat in two broken kitchen chairs outside, since he was about to turn eighty and was still taking special precautions because of his vulnerability to Covid. His eyes were watering in the inner corners, with thin drips darkening the creases of his wrinkled cheeks. We looked at the ashes, and he thumbed through the drawings and the photos. The red velvet pouch looked lush, but the ashes themselves were separated in plain bags, one for Jeremiah and one for Ciera. Those plastic bags upset him.

We spoke for an hour and a half, out there on the stoop. Nathaniel talked in his usual way, circling back to the children's lives with him while they were little, returning to the pain of his losing them, blaming Sherry for her bad behavior while simultaneously expressing his loyalty and devotion to her, even though she barely ever stopped by anymore. She was supposed to be his caretaker; she got some of his disability benefits for the task. But he could never get her to visit, let alone help him with things around the house or take him to appointments. His first wife, Rose, had been talking about moving him into her house, but she said she wouldn't do it while he was still married to Sherry. And although Nathaniel needed the help, and wanted the companionship, he couldn't bring himself to abandon Sherry.

He didn't want to abandon Dontay, either. Dontay was still staying out for days at a time, who knew where. When he came home, he slept all day or played video games until he passed out on the living room floor. Nathaniel tried hard to get Dontay's disability benefits going again, the benefits he'd received as a child for his mental illness but lost when he was incarcerated. Dontay still couldn't be bothered to attend the meetings Nathaniel set up for him and even went so far as to tell someone from the Social Security Administration when they called that he didn't want the money.

There was nothing Nathaniel could do; Dontay was an adult, after all. But a job seemed out of reach for him, and in Nathaniel's mind, if he could just get those disability benefits, Dontay might be all right. Nathaniel was old, after all, and tired.

His visits to the doctor had become more frequent, and doctors and nurses kept asking him why there was no one present with him at the appointments. One day earlier that winter, Nathaniel had had to go into the hospital for a medical procedure, one that required him to have someone with him to take him home afterward. He brought Dontay along, on the bus, but the procedure was delayed. Nathaniel said he waited nearly two hours in a room before the procedure even took place. After a while, he told the nurse to tell his son, in the waiting room, that he could go home. "Oh, he left a long time ago," the nurse told him.

When the procedure was finished, he couldn't get ahold of Dontay, or of Sherry, who increasingly ignored his calls. It was cold and raining, and the hospital wouldn't have let him leave on his own even if he wanted to brave the bus in that weather. After a while, he reached his brother, who came after several hours to pick him up.

Nathaniel was increasingly consumed with thoughts of the time he had left. His back hurt every day and his knees were often swollen. His stomach became distended, and he had problems chewing and digesting his food. He wanted peace and quiet, to enjoy the rest of his life. But instead, he sat there with me on the stoop, the one member of the Davis family who was able to face collecting the remains of the dead children. As he'd been proving for decades, through Dontay's torturous split from his siblings, his institutionalization, his incarceration, his bad behavior; and through a decades-long partnership with Dontay's mother, whose cocaine addiction ebbed and flowed but never ceased, who took his money and let him pay her rent but couldn't be counted on to show up or to help him get around, whose life was scarred by her mother's murder, who struggled to face the hard things . . . Nathaniel would show up. He didn't want to be like everyone else in their life, who left them behind, who gave up.

Lately, he had considered asking Sherry for a divorce, wavering back and forth between a loyalty to their marriage and a frustrated despair at her disregard of his need for help. He was embarrassed to be so old, when she still had so much life to live. He was embarrassed to need help doing the things he'd always been able to do on his own.

But with Dontay, there was no wavering. Nathaniel would be there. He wouldn't leave. He wouldn't give up on him. "It's not right. I want to go to heaven," he said. "If he knocks, I won't close the door on him."

Questions arose about what the family would do with the remains: Would they want to hold a memorial service? Or possibly have them interred somewhere? Maybe they could release them into the ocean, as Nathaniel considered, where they might be spiritually connected to their missing brother, Devonte.

"I really thank you for everything from the bottom of

my heart," Sherry wrote me in a text message. "I'm sorry I'm not ready to have a service for my babies. It's already hard for me that they took my kids and they are dead by another person who's supposed to love them. I haven't gotten over that and to try and give them another service will really break me down, I can't do that."

The questions caused a conflict in the Davis family. Dontay did not want to part with his siblings, and Sherry got extremely upset when she heard Nathaniel was thinking of scattering the ashes. Nathaniel settled on purchasing a silver-and-gold urn, and putting the two siblings' ashes in there, together.

In January 2021, I drove seven hours out to Mobile to deliver the ashes of Tammy's children to her. The loblolly pines of the Gulf Coast made way for the cypress swamps outside New Orleans, and by the time I reached Mobile it was mid-afternoon. I drove straight to Tammy's apartment, a cluster of buildings marred by construction as a beautification effort was under way.

She came out to my car to meet me, wearing a black T-shirt and black athletic pants, with black-and-gold Nikes. Her hair was dyed maroon, and she looked a bit different, maybe smaller than when I had seen her last, years before. She walked me back through the courtyard, among the half-finished buildings, to a stairwell that led up to the apartment she shared with Rob. He was inside, with Toto and their other mini Yorkie, Tinkerbell, Rob's pet. The dogs were tiny

and old, and immediately curled up on either side of me on
the couch. Rob was courteous, thanking me profusely, explaining how much it meant to Tammy. He was tender with
her, too, with a hand on her nearly constantly, although he
seemed to get on her nerves bumbling around a little bit.

The apartment was small, and the carpet was stained,
something Tammy pointed out angrily. They'd toured another
unit but ended up in this one, and since they were paying $400
a month and couldn't afford much more, they made do. They
took impeccable care of the apartment. Everything was neat
and tidy, and the kitchen had red counters and matching red
appliances. In the corner of the living room was a bouncy
chair, for the little boy, just about a year old, whom Tammy
had been watching for Rob's relatives.

She'd loved taking care of a baby again. She knew his
rhythms and laughed at his strength—he was a huge baby
and started walking early, so she had her hands full. The
child wasn't home now, but his things were scattered all
through the apartment.

She sat down on the couch with me and opened the album I had brought for her. It had a blue suede-like cover
on which red embroidery spelled out "Family"; I had found
it in Jennifer's things. The album was totally empty, except
for about ten pages in the back filled with photos of Markis,
Hannah, and Abigail when they were very young. These
photos were what came with the kids when they got adopted;
Tammy had the children with her then, and she remembered
the tiny details about where they were when each photo
was taken. In one, Markis wears a Spider-Man costume for

Halloween. Another shows a chubby-faced Markis celebrating his fourth birthday at Chuck E. Cheese. One depicts Hannah smiling widely at the bottom of a slide; the playground was at a church, Tammy remembers, and they were there with her friend Cynthia, who has since passed away.

I had filled the rest of the pages in the album with photos of the children that Jennifer had taken. It was clear looking through the photos that shortly after Devonte, Jeremiah, and Ciera were adopted, Jennifer switched from film to digital; many of the photos of them that were posted online do not exist in her physical archive. I had given the Davis family what record there was of their children, which wasn't much. But with the first three, there were many photos. Swimming in the lake in colorful bathing suits. Playing in the snow in bulky snowsuits. The three of them posed and smiling among the fall leaves. Hannah and Abigail, both with big grins, hugging each other. Little glimpses of girlish attitude, Hannah making a peace sign, Abigail sitting on her grandpa's lap, giving side-eye.

Tammy loved the photos, and looked at each one. When we reached the end, she showed me a picture of the urn she had picked out to hold her children, all together. She opened the red velvet pouch that contained her children's remains. She began crying heavily, Rob sitting on the other side of her, stroking her back. She held the bags in her hands, one at a time, closing her eyes.

Epilogue

For years, Tammy had gone through life without her front teeth. They'd been knocked out during a fight with her husband, and she had no money to replace them. For much of that time, she'd had no inkling that across the country, her first daughter, Hannah, was living her young life without her front teeth as well.

Tammy's teeth were a constant source of embarrassment for her. In 2021, when Rob's full disability benefits kicked in, he paid for her to replace them with dentures. She sent me several photos in which she is smiling broadly, her mouth open wide.

When Tammy looks at photos of Hannah, she says it's hard to recognize the tiny teen girl she knew only as a toddler. Even so, Tammy has never thought about the connection between her missing front teeth and Hannah's. She's been consumed with her own survival in the years since she lost Hannah and her siblings, clawing her way out of home-lessness and then riding the cresting and crashing waves of her volatile relationship.

But it's unsettling, the coincidence. I noticed it the first time Tammy and I met, and I was struck with the physical manifestation of a connection that had been tugging darkly at me since I started working on this story. Between mother's and daughter's stories runs a through line of abuse.

That's not unexpected for stories about the child welfare system, of course; the point of the system is to protect chil-dren from that kind of harm. But the Hart family story com-plicates popular narratives about abuse and the role of CPS in protecting children from it. The children's birth families were not beating their children or starving them; they were clearly struggling with substance use and mental illness, but instead of receiving help, the parents were punished. On the other hand, authorities consistently projected a halo of goodness onto the adoptive mothers, throughout a decade of abuse allegations and even after the murder of their children, with cops and other officials bending over backward to in-terpret their actions in the kindest possible light.

In stories about adoption in the media, we largely see through the eyes of the adoptive parents, who are given the central role. Their "journey" to adoption, the challenges they experience, and their awe-inspiring love for their kids are common themes—Jennifer didn't make up this narrative; in fact, many people related to it partially because it is the stan-dard one.

What is less common is to hear from the adoptees them-

selves, many of whom have complicated views on their experience. Multiple studies have shown that, compared with
children raised by their birth families, adoptees are at greater
risk of having mental health challenges, including depression, anxiety, and other mood disorders. Research has found
this correlation even for children adopted as infants, but additional studies have shown that children who were adopted
at older ages suffer from more behavioral and psychological
problems.

Like adoptees, birth mothers' stories are rarely told.

"The experience of being a birth mom is very isolating.
There's a lot of shame and a lot of guilt placed on women
who place their children for adoption or have lost children to
the child welfare system, shame that you're not able to be a
good mom, that you're not able to be a mother," says Robin
Endres, the director of MPower Alliance, the nonprofit that
helped Tammy access therapy during her mental health crisis
after she heard about her children's deaths.

Mothers caught up in the child welfare system are usually
already struggling, whether it be due to domestic violence
or substance use or mental illness. When the state steps in
and takes children from already struggling parents, that can
feel like a death blow to their self-image. "For the most part,
their lives get disrupted so much that it's hard for them to
ever feel completely safe," says Pearl Chen, also of MPower
Alliance. "They self-sabotage. When they get close to healing, they find ways to not trust it."

Sherry was still a child when she had a first child of her
own, and that child, DeMarcus, is now a grown man. Sherry

talks from time to time with her third child, DeQuince, but she still longs to find DeMarcus and his brother DeAndre, whose whereabouts are unknown. The experience of losing her first three boys to the child welfare system undoubtedly affected her relationships with her younger children. For Tammy, who had more children after Markis, Hannah, and Abigail, the trauma of losing her first three sealed her fate—and her self-image—as someone who was unable to parent.

The child welfare system didn't cause the trauma Tammy or Sherry experienced at a young age, but neither did it help them deal with it. The women's experiences with Child Protective Services added further trauma to their lives. Instead of getting help with taking her children to the hospital, Tammy got paperwork removing them from her care. Instead of creating a safety plan that would allow Sherry to see her children while they were in the care of their aunt, CPS disallowed all contact and punished the family so harshly when they disobeyed that the children were lost to the family forever.

The child-parent relationship is the most foundational bond of a person's life. Our society is organized around the nuclear family unit, and even when children need to be removed from their parents for their safety, losing access to family is a trauma in itself.

There are no perfect parents, and despite their best intentions, it is likely that parents will inflict some harm on their children. Even for parents who have enough money to meet their children's needs and more, parenting can still be fraught. The state's response to parental harm, though, is not meted out equally.

CPS has the duty to keep children safe, but the scales of harm are imbalanced. For one, in virtually all cases, CPS steps in when a family is already marginalized, whether by poverty, race, class, mental illness, drug use, disability, or LGBTQ or immigration status. Their offered support is implicitly or explicitly coercive, and the threat of removal to ensure compliance may leave parents in worse shape than they were before CPS entered their lives. Our punitive approach to families who likely need some form of help that the state is not willing to provide too often does nothing to help the children CPS is tasked with caring for.

Because, after all, CPS's duty is first and foremost to the child. In its duty to Dontay Davis—and to thousands of others like him who are in long-term foster care—the system failed and continues to fail miserably. Instead of love and kindness, kids like Dontay are met with oppressive institutions, where physical and sexual abuse is routine. Even without exhibiting traumatized behaviors, foster children experience multiple placement moves—one young woman who spent most of her childhood in institutions told me that the only foster family she felt happy and safe with lost the ability to care for her when their child placing agency changed; for this bureaucratic reason, a childhood sexual abuse survivor was shuttled away from the only bond she'd made in foster care and into a series of violent and scary group homes. When Dontay lost contact with his siblings, he became suicidal and depressed. But his therapists didn't earn his trust enough for him to open up to them; instead, he was heavily medicated, and sometimes even tranquilized, which traumatized him to the extent that, as an adult, he refuses to take the medication he needs or even go to the doctor.

In 2020, a major international review of published research found that more than six million children are living in institutions worldwide, and recommended that institutional care of children should be phased out completely. "Institutions provide suboptimal care and are associated with substantial developmental delays in physical growth, cognition, attention, socioemotional development and mental health," wrote the authors of the study, which was commissioned by the UK-based *Lancet*. In the United States, the overall use of institutional care has declined, but an analysis by child welfare news organization *The Imprint* found that in twenty states, the number of foster youth in institutions rose between 2011 and 2017, and in half of those states, the number rose by at least 20 percent. And crucially, placements in residential treatment centers require children to be designated as requiring high levels of care, making them much, much less likely to get adopted. Teens who are institutionalized often run away, and are more likely than other teens to become homeless, engage in survival sex work, and be incarcerated.

Kelis Houston used to work in the central intake shelter in Minneapolis, Minnesota. It was there that she noticed that virtually all the children were Black. "A lot of them came back to us three and four times a year, because they were being placed in culturally inappropriate homes, different treatment facilities. A lot ended up in juvenile detention and then just came back to us. It was just this cycle that I saw these children experience until they aged out of the system without permanency," Kelis says. "While they're placed in these shelters and different facilities and foster homes, they're getting these rap sheets, where on paper they look like just these horrible delinquents, when really this is just a child that needs mental health services and support and some sort of safe adult."

Kelis has attempted to tackle this problem through legislation called the Minnesota African American Family Preservation Act, which she helped write and has been pushing to pass since 2018—so far unsuccessfully. The bill would require caseworkers to make "active efforts" to reunify Black children with their families, engage families in home-based services prior to removing Black children from their care, and limit removals of Black children to cases in which they are in immediate danger of harm. State representative Esther Agbaje, who sponsored the bill during the 2021 session, said the foundational concepts were modeled after the Indian Child Welfare Act, which provides specific protections to children affiliated with a Native American tribe.

But even ICWA, a law that has been roundly praised by child welfare advocacy groups and whose central tenets of family preservation are now widely considered best practice across the field, has been challenged in the courts numerous times. In the 2018 Texas case *Brackeen v. Haaland*, the latest serious challenge, the Fifth Circuit Court issued a

ruling in 2021 that limited aspects of ICWA in certain jurisdictions. In early 2022, the Supreme Court announced it
would hear the *Brackeen* case.

Whatever its fate, ICWA stands on sturdier legal ground
than a law that would apply to Black children. The central
legal argument in defense of ICWA builds on the tribes' status as sovereign nations and not as a race. Potential laws in
which classifications are based on race must adhere to the
legal standard of "strict scrutiny," which is a notoriously difficult standard to meet; the well-known adage "strict in theory, fatal in fact" alludes to the likelihood that these types of
laws will be struck down. Because of this, Black activists will
likely have a hard time ensuring that a law protecting Black
children in the foster care system can hold up in the courts.

Steps are being taken to expand some of the rights that
ICWA guarantees to all children in the child welfare system.
In 2022, the Washington State supreme court ruled that a
meaningful preference must be given to a child's relatives—
even when the child's rights to a parent have been terminated.
In the case in question, the Washington State Department
of Children, Youth & Families had argued that when children's ties to their mothers are severed, the law requiring a
preference for placing children with relatives was no longer
relevant. The court strongly disagreed: "Disrupting a child's
placement, as happened in this case, for reasons that appear
to have virtually no grounds at all, creates chaos for the
child," the opinion states. "Courts *must* afford meaningful
preference to placement with relatives."

In the history of child welfare policy, "race-neutral" reforms have been the ones likely to become law. One such initiative would help both those who are at risk of entering the system and those who are aging out of it. The idea is simple, really: give money to those who need it. During the Covid-19 pandemic, an expansion of the Child Tax Credit was passed, giving most families a monthly stipend of $250 to $300 per child. Unlike welfare programs that require an extensive application process and are time-limited, the Child Tax Credit was relatively easy to receive and did not require proving one had an income below certain limits. Research found that the number of children living in poverty dropped by three million in a month and a half—cutting the child poverty rate by a third. The number of adults reporting that their family did not have enough to eat also dropped by a third. Despite these incredible effects, Congress let the Child Tax Credit expire at the end of 2021.

That same year, California passed a new law giving thousands of foster youth who age out of the state's care up to $1,000 per month for a year. The move constitutes the first statewide universal basic income, given to eligible young adults without restrictions. Foster youth across the country who age out of the system face abysmal outcomes. They often lack emotional or monetary family support and are saddled with the trauma of their long stays in foster care. Many aged-out youth experience homelessness. Advocates see this new law as a buffer for these young people, helping them achieve independence.

Some advocates—like Alan Dettlaff, the dean of the University of Houston Graduate School of Social Work and the director of the upEND Movement—want to push that thought further. "We remove kids for neglect and place them in strangers' homes, and give the stranger a monthly stipend to take care of the child," Dettlaff says. "What if we just gave that one thousand dollars a month to the mother who needed it?"

Traditionally, reforms in child welfare have been said to swing on a pendulum, from policies that favor family preservation to more hard-line "better safe than sorry" approaches. The swings toward removing more children have historically followed headline-making tragedies in which children were killed or seriously harmed by their birth parents' abuse. But as research increasingly shows that the act of removing a child from their parents is a trauma in and of itself, calls have gotten louder to weigh that impact against whatever trauma might be experienced by the child in their home.

During the 2021 Texas legislative session, a bipartisan majority of an otherwise deeply divided legislature passed a major reform of the Texas Family Code—the reform makes it much harder to remove a child for issues of neglect, which advocates say is often just another word for poverty. Republicans were some of the staunchest supporters of the legislation. The same is true for the Family First Prevention Services Act, passed during the Trump administration in 2018. The law frees up significant federal money for the first time to be directed toward preventive services, which have the goal of keeping children in their homes. The law also limits the federal money going to institutional settings for children, increases the requirements such places must meet to receive federal support, and drastically reduces the amount of time a child can receive such support, with the aim of shortening children's stays in restrictive treatment centers.

But reforms that seemed pretty radical in 2018 have not kept pace with the changing conversations about the child welfare system, which were pushed far past the traditional pendulum in the wake of 2020's Black Lives Matter uprisings. "As protests erupted around the nation and the world in response to continued police violence against Black people, the call to defund police and abolish prisons began to make more and more sense to more and more people," said Dorothy Roberts at a conference at Columbia University that took place twenty years after the publication of her book *Shattered Bonds: The Color of Child Welfare*. "The family policing system is part of that same carceral regime, and like the police and prison systems, family policing is designed to maintain racial injustice by punishing families in place of meeting their needs."

Roberts said that after the publication of *Shattered Bonds*, she was part of a task force impaneled in response to a class action lawsuit against Washington State for the failures of its child welfare system. She spent nine years working with a team of experts to develop a plan to reform the state's foster care system and to measure its progress. The nearly decade of work resulted in minimal improvements, she says, and the experience was demoralizing. "I think that the children's attorneys had good intentions; they wanted to end these horrible situations for children in foster care. And our panel had good intentions; we wanted to improve foster care. But it can't be fixed that way—it can't be fixed at all, is my conclusion."

A central tenet of abolition, whether of police and prisons or of the child welfare system, is the pursuit of "nonreformist reforms"—new policies that shrink, rather than grow, the reach of abusive systems, divesting from punishment models and investing in actual, community-led supports. Direct monetary transfers to those at risk or involved in the system fit the model, because it is not so much a reform to the child welfare system as it is support that is *untethered* from that system. On the other hand, providing more money for prevention services along the lines of Family First, Roberts said, only increases the overall budgets of a system that provides services to families only on the condition of surveillance and punishment for noncompliance.

The call to move beyond reforming the current child welfare system is gaining steam among some of the more well-known and well-regarded experts in child welfare. The former head of the Children's Bureau under Trump, Jerry Milner, is advising local child welfare agencies that are undertaking total overhauls of their systems, with the goal of "radical change and wholesale replacement of the current system," he says, one that "was never established to support families." The first such project will be based in Little Rock, Arkansas.

It can be hard for the average person to wrap their heads around abolition of the system—after all, domestic violence happens, and children can be and sometimes are horrifically abused. Many of the safeguards that would prevent such abuse from happening—including increased access to substance abuse treatment, mental and physical health care, and housing assistance—do not yet exist. The idea requires a radical reimagining of what support for parents looks like, and it calls for something even more difficult for many to embrace: a release of the urge to judge and blame parents and of wanting to punish them for their failures. In a society that resorts to individual punishment as a response to many of its systemic ills, this concept is deeply embedded into our psyches, and it is hard to let go.

In our current approach to child welfare, we see children as distinct from their parents, and often at odds with them. For young children, we hope to save them by whisking them away to a safe and stable home, far away from the chaos of their upbringing. For older children, who have been stuck in the system longer, we pathologize them for their rational responses to a life of instability, of fractured bonds, of survival. We tell these children they must renounce their families in order to have a chance at a "better life." But children both young and older exist in the context of their own families, their own histories.

What initially drew me to reporting on foster care was a level of personal understanding about the long-term effects of child abuse and neglect. As a survivor of child sexual abuse outside the home, and living in a fractured family that often left me to fend for myself, I understood the destabilizing effect of abuse on one's psyche and individual choices well into adulthood.

Although my friends and I were often left unsupervised as our parents struggled with abusive partners or substance abuse or mental illness, the involvement of CPS in our lives was so far from a possibility it didn't even factor into our or our parents' decision-making. We as children and teens certainly never considered that we might encounter CPS. I thought about this a lot as I learned about how the system interacts with families: The harm I experienced was real—I struggle with PTSD to this day. But would it have helped for me to have been separated from my friends, my school, the sources of stability in my life? Would it have helped if I had been made to stay away from my family, split up from my siblings? And why, as a middle-class white person, did I never have to worry about that happening, when every day Black families are making parenting decisions with the threat of government intervention looming over them?

The profound inequities at play allowed me to move on from my childhood relatively unscathed, and I realize now that so many other children aren't given the opportunities, and the safety from the constant traumas of poverty and of racism, to do the same. Despite the chaos at home, I had crucial community support: my high school boyfriend's parents, at whose dinner table I was always welcome; my favorite teacher, who kept an eye on me and gave my life structure; a tight-knit group of best friends who helped one another through the ups and downs of our unstable home lives.

Each child deserves a safe place to call home. So, too, do they deserve a community of people who love them, who care for them, and who step in when their own parents can't. This should be the standard of care each child receives. In this respect, we are failing far too many.

Notes

Prologue

3 *A man and his wife*: Many of the details in this section come from the investigative documents and the inquest into the Hart family's deaths. Hart Family Coroner's Inquest – Day 1, Mendocino County Sheriff's Office, streamed live on April 3, 2019, by YouTube user MendocinoSheriff, https://www.youtube.com/watch?v=H37dIwNQ6I0; Hart Family Coroner's Inquest – Day 2, Mendocino County Sheriff's Office, streamed live on April 4, 2019, by YouTube user MendocinoSheriff, https://www.youtube.com/watch?v=ULL-TAAlFQU.

5 *a violent altercation*: Kym Kemp, "Shooting Victim Still Beat Suspect with a Shovel, Says Mendocino Sheriff's Department," *Redheaded BlackBelt*, March 29, 2018, kymkemp.com/2018/03/29/shooting-victim-still-beat-suspect-with-shovel-says-mendocino-sheriffs-department/.

8 *"We have no evidence"*: Tom Allman, quoted in Shane Dixon Kavanaugh, "Child in Viral Portland Police Hug Photo Missing, 5 Family Members Dead After California Cliff Crash," *The Oregonian*, March 28, 2018.

10 *viral photo*: Emanuella Grinberg, "The Hug Shared Around the World," CNN, December 1, 2014.

1. "Every Time I See You, You Take Me Away"

13 *It was a mild December day*: Much of the primary documentation for this chapter and chapter 2 comes from the complete foster care case file of Dontay Davis.

16 *$350 for each child*: Marissa Evans, "Texas Senate Approves Monthly Payments for Relative Caregivers of Abused Children," *Texas Tribune*, May 22, 2017.

16 *kinship placements*: H. L. Whitman, "Letter to Caregivers," Commissioner of Department of Family and Protective Services, September 1, 2017.

20 *Rose lived with her boyfriend*: Details of Rose's murder come from the Houston Police Department's investigative file of the case.

25 *shut down in 2012*: "Psychiatric Hospital Forced to Close," Click 2Houston.com, January 31, 2014, www.click2houston.com/news /2012/01/31/psychiatric-hospital-forced-to-close/.

26 *almost 348,000*: Stephen M. Ryan, "Texas Foster Care: Current Issues, Reform Efforts and Remaining Problems," *Texas Appleseed*, September 2007.

26 *a scathing report*: Carole Keeton Strayhorn, "Forgotten Children," Report of the Texas Comptroller, 2004.

27 *In 2005, the Texas legislature*: Ryan, "Texas Foster Care."

2. A Safe Place

34 *ASFA triggers a timeline*: Dorothy Roberts, *Shattered Bonds: The Color of Child Welfare* (New York: Basic Books, 2002), 104–12.

34 *"permanent, stable homes"*: *Congressional Record* 143, no. 160 (Thursday, November 13, 1997), House of Representatives, H10776–H10790 (statement of Representative Deborah Pryce).

35 *More than one million*: Kim Phagan-Hansel, "One Million Adop-

tions Later: The Adoption and Safe Families Act at 20," *The Imprint: Youth & Family News*, November 28, 2018.

35 *a wave of more than two million*: Martin Guggenheim, "Let's Root Out Racism in Child Welfare, Too," *The Imprint: Youth & Family News*, June 15, 2020.

35 *2.4 times more likely*: Christopher Wildeman, Frank R. Edwards, and Sara Wakefield, "The Cumulative Prevalence of Termination of Parental Rights for U.S. Children," *Child Maltreatment* 25, no. 1 (February 2020): 32–42; and Christina White, "Federally Mandated Destruction of the Black Family: The Adoption and Safe Families," *Northwestern Journal of Law and Social Policy* 1, no. 1 (2006): 303–37.

3. The Good Ol' Boys Club

43 *When Shelton took the bench*: Tim Fleck, "Bully on the Bench," *Houston Press*, July 1, 1999. Much of the historical detail about Shelton in the ensuing paragraphs comes from this story.

44 *DA John Holmes Jr.*: John Holmes Jr., "Dealing Out Death," *Texas Monthly*, July 2002.

45 *"the acknowledged king"*: Mary Flood, "The King and His Courts," *Houston Press*, August 29, 1996.

45 *with the support of Steve Hotze*: Tim Fleck, "The Kingdom and the Power," *Houston Press*, October 3, 1996. Much of the historical detail about Steve Hotze in the ensuing paragraphs comes from this story.

46 *Hotze spent the ensuing decades*: Erin Douglas, "Former Houston Police Captain Accused of Violent Attempt to Prove Election Conspiracy Was Hired by GOP Activist's Group," *Texas Tribune*, December 15, 2020.

46 *"I want to make sure"*: Steve Hotze, quoted in Patrick Svitek, "'Kill 'Em': Houston GOP Powerbroker Steve Hotze Left Greg Abbott a Voicemail Requesting That National Guard 'Shoot to Kill' Rioters," *Texas Tribune*, July 3, 2020.

49 *"Family destruction has historically functioned"*: Dorothy Roberts, *Torn Apart: How the Child Welfare System Destroys Black Families—And How Abolition Can Build a Safer World* (New York: Basic Books, 2022), 87.

49 *"Steeped in Victorian gender ideals"*: Margaret D. Jacobs, "Remembering the 'Forgotten Child': The American Indian Child Welfare Crisis of the 1960s and 1970s," in "Native Adoption in Canada, the United States, New Zealand, and Australia," special issue, *American Indian Quarterly* 37, no. 1–2 (Spring 2013): 139.

50 *"immersing the Indian in our civilization"*: Speech by Richard Henry Pratt, 1892, Carlisle Indian School Digital Resource Center, https://carlisleindian.dickinson.edu/teach/kill-indian-him-and-save-man-r-h-pratt-education-native-americans. Following Pratt quote also sourced from this speech.

50 *"Child-saving advocates"*: Roberts, *Torn Apart*, 113.

51 *in 1931, only 3 percent*: Linda Gordon, *Pitied But Not Entitled: Single Mothers and the History of Welfare, 1890–1935* (Cambridge, MA: Harvard University Press, 1994), 48.

51 *the battered child*: Mical Raz, *Abusive Policies: How the American Child Welfare System Lost Its Way* (Chapel Hill: University of North Carolina Press, 2020), 3.

51 *continued to balloon*: "Children's Bureau Timeline," Child Welfare Information Gateway, www.childwelfare.gov/more-tools-resources/resources-from-childrens-bureau/timeline1/.

52 *double whammy*: Laura Meyer and Ife Floyd, "Cash Assistance Should Reach Millions More Families to Lessen Hardship: Families' Access Limited by Policies Rooted in Racism," policy brief, Center on Budget and Policy Priorities, November 2020.

52 *twice as likely*: Stephen M. Ryan, "Texas Foster Care: Current Issues, Reform Efforts and Remaining Problems," *Texas Appleseed*, September 2007.

53 *"I'm not saying Pat Shelton"*: Fleck, "Bully on the Bench."

54 *"Anybody who speaks to you*: Fleck, "Bully on the Bench."

55 *Texas was and continues to be an exception*: Christie Renick, "Bigger

in Texas: Number of Adoptions, and Parents Who Lose Their Rights," *The Imprint: Youth & Family News*, May 24, 2018.

56 *Shelton's nineteen-year-old daughter*: Brian Rogers, "Judge's Daughter in Court After Fatal Accident," *Houston Chronicle*, October 25, 2006. Much of the material about Elizabeth Shelton's accident was sourced additionally from the Houston Police Department investigation file, obtained through a public records request.

56 *"My daddy is a"*: Elizabeth Shelton, quoted in "Did Judge's Daughter Get Special Treatment?," ABC13 Eyewitness News, March 5, 2009.

56 *Mark Sandoval*: Rick Casey, "Judge Sure Keeps This Lawyer Busy," *Houston Chronicle*, October 17, 2007.

56 *Sandoval went to the public*: Peggy O'Hare, "Evidence Tampering Alleged at Trial of Shelton," *Houston Chronicle*, October 5, 2007.

57 *The sheriff's office told*: Brian Rogers, "Judge's Daughter Sees Penalty Changed in DWI Death," *Houston Chronicle*, March 6, 2009.

59 *The state earned nearly $8.5 million*: "Adoption and Legal Guardianship Incentive Payment Program—Earning History by State: FY 1998–FY 2019, Administration for Children and Families, www.acf.hhs.gov/sites/default/files/documents/cb/adoption_incentives_earning_history_2020.pdf.

59 *aside from continuing to send monthly payments*: Allie Morris, "Six Children Involved in Fatal California Crash Adopted from Houston Area," *San Antonio Express-News*, April 6, 2018.

4. "Big-Time Small-Time Living"

64 *currently serving a life sentence*: South Dakota Department of Corrections Offender Locator, https://doc.sd.gov/adult/lookup/.

64 *Wilson was a twenty-eight-year-old*: Staff reports, "Homicide Cases Not New to Aberdeen Area," *Aberdeen News*, January 13, 2015.

64 *"We put in statutory law"*: David W. Dunlap, "Fearing a Toehold for Gay Marriages, Conservatives Rush to Bar the Door," *New York*

Times, March 6, 1996. The following quote, by Barry Wick, is also sourced from this story.

5. Across State Lines

77 *"Most touching of all"*: Charles Loring Brace, *The Dangerous Classes of New York and Twenty Years' Work Among Them* (New York: Wynkoop & Hallenbeck, 1872), 88–89.

78 *"These boys and girls"*: Brace, *The Dangerous Classes*, 92.

78 *"We hope, too"*: Brace, *The Dangerous Classes*, 92.

79 *"orphan trains"*: Angelique Brown, "Orphan Trains (1854–1929)," Social Welfare History Project, 2011, socialwelfare.library.vcu .edu/programs/child-welfarechild-labor/orphan-trains/.

79 *"Some ordered boys"*: Nebraska paper, 1912, quoted in Andrea Warren, "The Orphan Train," *Washington Post*, November 11, 1998.

79 *People raising other people's children*: Much of the history in this section is sourced from the Adoption History Project, pages .uoregon.edu/adoption/about.html, created and maintained by Ellen Herman in the Department of History at the University of Oregon.

80 *"The Compact"*: "ICPC FAQ's," American Public Human Services Association, https://aphsa.org/AAICPC/AAICPC/icpc_faq_2 .aspx.

80 *Concurrent planning*: Carolyn Lipp, "Fostering Uncertainty?: A Critique of Concurrent Planning in the Child Welfare System," *Family Law Quarterly* 52, no. 1 (Spring 2018): 221–43.

6. "If Not Us, Who?"

87 *1.5 million babies*: Ann Fessler, *The Girls Who Were Sent Away: The Hidden History of Women Who Surrendered Children for Adoption in the Decades Before* Roe v. Wade (New York: Penguin Press, 2006), 8.

87 *"agencies adopted a powerful"*: Elizabeth Bartholet, "Where Do Black Children Belong? The Politics of Race Matching in Adop-

tion," *University of Pennsylvania Law Review* 39, no. 5 (May 1991):
1176.

88   *"It was almost as if"*: Laura Briggs, *Somebody's Children: The Politics of
Transnational and Transracial Adoption* (Durham, NC: Duke University Press, 2012), 35.

89   *"During the past decade"*: Arnold Lyslo, quoted in Margaret D.
Jacobs, "Remembering the 'Forgotten Child': The American
Indian Child Welfare Crisis of the 1960s and 1970s," in "Native
Adoption in Canada, the United States, New Zealand, and Aus-
tralia," special issue, *American Indian Quarterly* 37, no. 1–2 (Spring
2013): 143.

89   *One study by the psychologist*: Joseph Westermeyer, "The Ravage of
Indian Families in Crisis," in *The Destruction of American Indian
Families*, ed. Steven Unger (New York: Association on American
Indian Affairs, 1977), 47–56.

89   *"One little, two little"*: "Adoptions of Indian Children Increase,"
press release, Bureau of Indian Affairs, April 14, 1966.

90   *"some agencies and social workers"*: Briggs, *Somebody's Children*, 36.

90   *"Trans-racial adoption of Black children"*: "National Association of
Black Social Workers Position Statement on Trans-Racial Adoptions," September 1972, cdn.ymaws.com/www.nabsw.org/resource
/collection/E1582D77-E4CD-4104-996A-D42D08F9CA7D
/NABSW_Trans-Racial_Adoption_1972_Position_(b).pdf.

91   *"The resolution was not based"*: Leora Neal, quoted in Briggs, *Somebody's Children*, 28.

91   *"the systematic court-ordered displacement"*: Dorothy Roberts, *Torn
Apart: How the Child Welfare System Destroys Black Families—And
How Abolition Can Build a Safer World* (New York: Basic Books,
2022), 97.

92   *"requiring due consideration"*: Minority Child Heritage Protection
Act, quoted in Wright S. Walling, "Adoption Law in Minnesota:
A Historical Perspective," *William Mitchell Law Review* 33, no. 3
(2007): 889.

92   *"It is true, as advocates"*: Bartholet, "Where Do Black Children Belong?," 1256.

93 *"It seems to me clear"*: Elizabeth Bartholet, "Cultural Stereotypes Can and Do Die: It's Time to Move On with Transracial Adoption," *Journal of the American Academy of Psychiatry and the Law* 34, no. 3 (2006): 320.

93 *But that doesn't mean*: Melissa Guida-Richards, *What White Parents Should Know About Transracial Adoption: An Adoptee's Perspective on Its History, Nuances, and Practices* (Berkeley, CA: North Atlantic Books, 2021), 16–23.

8. "Is It Because I'm Bad?"

108 *The problem of what to do*: Much of the history in this section of the chapter was informed by Kenneth Wooden, *Weeping in the Playtime of Others: America's Incarcerated Children* (Columbus: Ohio State University Press, 1976).

109 *A statute was enacted*: "The Greatest Reform School in the World: A Guide to the Records of the New York House of Refuge," New York State Archives, 1989, www.archives.nysed.gov/common/archives/files/res_topics_ed_reform.pdf.

109 *adopted a mental health focus*: Martin Leichtman, "Residential Treatment of Children and Adolescents: Past, Present, and Future," *American Journal of Orthopsychiatry* 76, no. 3 (2006): 285–94.

111 *"bullied, awed, and terrorized"*: [Name withheld], "Brutal Bettelheim," letter to the editor, *Chicago Reader*, April 5, 1990. (This letter was later credited to Alida Jatich, who was a resident for seven years at Bettelheim's school.)

111 *"dope addicts and prostitutes"*: Lester Roloff, quoted in Pamela Colloff, "Remember the Christian Alamo," *Texas Monthly*, December 2001. Other quotes about the Rebekah Home in this and the following paragraphs are from this article.

113 *the term "foster homes"*: Elizabeth Kolbert, "The Vocabulary of Votes: Frank Luntz," *New York Times Magazine*, March 26, 1995.

113 *"In baseball terms"*: Frank Luntz, quoted in "The Power of Words," editorial, *Washington Post*, February 4, 1995.

113 *Each day in 2019*: Mark M. Chatfield et al., "Quality of Experience in Residential Care Programmes: Retrospective Perspectives of Former Youth Participants," *Child & Family Social Work* 26, no. 2 (September 2020): 132–43.

117 *when an allegation of abuse is made*: M.D. ex rel Stukenberg v. Abbott, No. 2:11-cv-84, First Court Monitors' Report 2020, www.txs .uscourts.gov/sites/txs/files/869-main_0.pdf.

9. Dichotomy

126 *"profoundly disrespectful to Islam"*: Brett Campbell, "Beloved Festival Works Toward Providing a Truly Diverse Experience," *The Oregonian*, August 6, 2019.

127 *A concertgoer's video recording*: "Xavier Rudd Messages/Guku~ 'Xaviers Free Hug' @ Beloved Festival 2013," uploaded by You-Tube user Peaceful Ventures on March 8, 2014. https://www .youtube.com/watch?v=xQx_ypnpIO0.

131 *"A young boy who was born"*: Chloe Johnson, "Meet Devonte: The Little Boy with a Big Heart," *Huffington Post*, November 13, 2014.

133 *"People saw what they wanted to see"*: Isabel Wilkerson, *Caste: The Origins of Our Discontents* (New York: Random House, 2020).

135 *"They whip us with a belt"*: Hannah Hart, quoted in Lauren Smiley, "Two White Moms. Six Black Kids. One Unthinkable Tragedy. A Look Inside the 'Perfect' Hart Family," *Glamour*, September 6, 2018. Many of the details in this section of the chapter are from this article.

10. "Kiss Your Mama"

144 *a study by the Association of Indian Affairs reported*: Report to the 95th Congress, 2nd Session, "Establishing Standards for the Placement of Indian Children in Foster or Adoptive Homes, to Prevent the Breakup of Indian Families, and for Other Purposes," July 24, 1978, 9.

13. "Something I Could Love Unconditionally"

198 *Qualitative research has shown*: Abigail Dunn et al., "The Parenting Experience of Those with Borderline Personality Disorder Traits: Practitioner and Parent Perspectives," *Frontiers in Psychology*, August 7, 2020.

14. "Death at the Hands of Another"

210 *"This is the first coroner's inquest"*: Tom Allman, quoted in Justine Frederiksen, "Mendocino County Sheriff's Office Schedules Inquest into Hart Family Crash," *Ukiah Daily Journal*, March 21, 2019.

211 *The Hart family's story got the true crime treatment*: See Justine Harman, Liz Egan, and Lauren Smiley, "Broken Harts," eight-part podcast produced by *Glamour* and How Stuff Works, December 4, 2018–January 29, 2019, www.glamour.com/about/broken-harts.

215 *"decline in socializing"*: Harvey Warren, "Far-Reaching Ramifications of Same-Sex Marriage and Adoption," *Laurel (MS) Leader Call*, June 1, 2018.

215 *"At one time"*: Nancy Polikoff, "Yes, Jennifer and Sarah Hart Played the Lesbian Card," *Beyond (Straight and Gay) Marriage* (blog), August 1, 2018, beyondstraightandgaymarriage.blogspot.com/2018/08/yes-sarah-and-jennifer-hart-played.html.

217 *"Can 500mg of Benadryl"*: Testimony of California Highway Patrol Officer Jay Slates, Hart Family Coroner's Inquest – Day 2, Mendocino County Sheriff's Office, streamed live on April 4, 2019, by YouTube user MendocinoSheriff, https://www.youtube.com/watch?v=ULL-TAAlFQU.

219 *"In my opinion"*: Testimony of Mendocino County Sheriff's Deputy Shannon Barney, Hart Family Coroner's Inquest – Day 2, Mendocino County Sheriff's Office, streamed live on April 4, 2019, by YouTube user MendocinoSheriff, https://www.youtube.com/watch?v=ULL-TAAlFQU.

220 *a six-month analysis of news reports*: Marty Langley, "American Rou-

lette: Murder-Suicide in the United States," Violence Policy Center, 7th ed., July 2020, vpc.org/studies/amroul2020.pdf.

220 *"Family annihilators"*: Taylor Oathout, "Family Annihilators: The Psychological Profiles of Murderous Fathers" (honors thesis, University at Albany, State University of New York, 2020), scholarsarchive.library.albany.edu/cgi/viewcontent.cgi?article =1022&context=honorscollege_cj.

15. Best Interests of the Child

225 *A 2018* Texas Tribune *report*: Neena Satija, "Harris County Juvenile Judges and Private Attorneys Accused of Cronyism: 'Everybody Wins but the Kids,'" *Texas Tribune*, November 1, 2018.

226 *In the 2010s*: Keri Blakinger, "2 Harris County Judges Responsible for 1 in 5 Children Sent to State Juvenile Prisons," *Houston Chronicle*, October 20, 2018.

226 *In one 2008 case*: Lisa Falkenberg, "Judge in 'Angela' Case Is Poster Child for Perils of Straight-Ticket Voting," *Houston Chronicle*, October 28, 2014; and Lisa Falkenberg, "Justice Denied for 13 Year Old Rape Victim," *Houston Chronicle*, December 11, 2013.

228 *"simply asking the kids"*: Keri Blakinger, "Promise Not to Kill Anyone? After Losing Election, TX Judge Wholesale Releases Juvenile Defendants," *Houston Chronicle*, November 7, 2018.

228 *Research has shown*: Mikkel Mertz and Signe Hald Andersen, "The Hidden Cost of Foster-Care: New Evidence on the Inter-Generational Transmission of Foster-Care Experiences," *British Journal of Social Work* 47 (2017): 1377–93.

243 *"It is as if a police department"*: Josh Gupta-Kagan, "America's Hidden Foster Care System," *Stanford Law Review* 72 (April 2020): 843.

16. A Final Resting Place

247 *Brenda had been quoted just once*: Will Callan, "Telling Lies: How a Decade of Deception Led to the Hart Family's Tragic End on the Mendocino Coast," *Sonoma Magazine*, November 2018.

Epilogue

272 *"Institutions provide suboptimal care"*: Marinus H. van IJzendoorn et al., "Institutionalisation and Deinstitutionalisation of Children 1: A Systematic and Integrative Review of Evidence Regarding Effects on Development," *The Lancet Psychiatry* 7, no. 8 (2020): 703–20. Quote here is from the press release announcing the review.

Acknowledgments

I am deeply grateful for the many people who have had a hand in the making of this book. First and foremost, I thank Nathaniel, Dontay, Tammy, Sherry, Peaches, and Ye for opening their hearts and lives to me. I'm grateful to Doug Hart for his desire to do right by the birth families, and for helping me to make it happen. I owe a huge debt of gratitude to Shane Dixon Kavanaugh and Andre Meunier at *The Oregonian*, as well as Molly Young and Everton Bailey. Without Shane's reaching out to me on a breaking news assignment, none of this would have happened, and the whole team did amazing early work on this case.

I am also incredibly grateful to Cassi Feldman and Simone Sebastian, two great editors who helped shepherd the initial stories about the birth families; Ethan Brown, who was one of the first champions of this story, and who helped in crucial ways throughout the process; John Kelly, one of the most knowledgeable journalists on child welfare policy in this country, for the chance to dig deeper into Texas foster care and for the valuable feedback; Andrea Kszystyniak for their incredibly sensitive and perceptive impressions of a draft; and Leon and Liza Soares, who kept me out of (too much) trouble in high school and have cheered me on ever since.

I couldn't have done this without my family: my mom, Laura, who was a reliable ear for my many worries and feelings about the story; my brother, Cameron, and sister, Mitra, for their thoughtful advice; and my dad, Andy, for starting me out (very) early on Jack London and Anton Chekhov.

Thanks also to my editor, Alex Star, who made this book better; Colin Dickerman, who took a chance on the idea; my agent, Mackenzie Brady Watson, for the support at each and every stage; and my copy editor, Janet Renard. Thanks always to my support team: my Day Ones, Ashley Shearer, Charmaine Pullman, and Sanja Nedeljkovic, for everything; Pia Agrawal and Carrie Schneider for their wise counsel; my generous buddies Ian Chant and Garrett Arnold for the help along the way; and Bijan Shafiei-Rad and Mario De Leon for the recovery hangs in Austin. Special thanks to Mark and Emma, at whose beautiful guest home, Club Alegria, much of this book was written. To my therapist, Beatriz Craven, and my trauma therapist, Robyn Gruber: Y'all are the real MVPs.

A special thank-you to the innumerable sources, experts, attorneys, people with lived experience, and advocates who have spoken to me about foster care over the years. And to Dorothy Roberts and Nina Bernstein, whose foundational texts helped me grasp the big picture, and whose personal kindnesses have been so meaningful to me; to the journalists whose work helped inform this one, including Tim Fleck, Rick Casey, Lisa Falkenberg, Keri Blakinger, Lauren Smiley, Kenneth Wooden, Richard Wexler, and many others; and to the CUNY Newmark Graduate School of Journalism, for the nuts-and-bolts lessons and for the connections to multiple people listed here, without whom this book would not be possible.

To my son, Rocco: Thank you for being the light of my life, for teaching me so much about all of it, and for being a good sport when your mom had to work. And, most crucially, to my husband, Paul DeBenedetto: You helped me fact-check this book, you shouldered the load for the hard parts, and you stood beside me as I traveled the depths of despair; a thank-you is not enough. I love you.